BLATANT
RAW FOODIST
PROPAGANDA!

Blatant Raw Foodist Propaganda!

or

SELL YOUR STOVE TO THE JUNKMAN AND FEEL GREAT!

or

CONSIDER YOUR TRUE NATURE

Joe Alexander

Blue Dolphin Publishing

Copyright © 1990 Joe Alexander
All rights reserved.*

*However, you are encouraged to quote this book liberally, so that
as many people as possible may hear about these ideas. You are also
encouraged to read the book out loud to your lover, family, friends,
acquaintances and total strangers. Take this book to foreign
countries, and leave it on park benches, art galleries and coffee
shops. In fact, please do anything you can to make the world a
better place to live, and the people in it happier, healthier and more
loving.

Permissions to quote passages from other books and articles were
solicited over three years. Very few were obtained. Raw foodists
move around a lot, and their writings do not seem to endure (see
Bibliography). Of the few who responded, we would like to thank
Ann Wigmore, Dick Gregory, and Bruce Last (Ehret Literature
Publishing) for allowing the use of quotations from previously
published material. To any other authors who may see this book and
feel slighted, please write the Author, c/o the Publisher, and we will
supply the proper credit in the next printing. Morris Krok . . .
where are you, anyway?

Excerpt from *Dick Gregory's Natural Diet for Folks Who Eat: Cooking
with Mother Nature* by Dick Gregory. Copyright © 1973 by Richard
Claxton Gregory. Reprinted by permission of HarperCollins
Publishers.

First Enlarged and Revised Edition, October 4, 1990

For information, address:
Blue Dolphin Publishing, Inc.
P.O. Box 1908, Nevada City, CA 95959

Published by special arrangement with
Pelican Pond Publishing, Nevada City, California
"Mens sana in corpore sano"

ISBN: 0-931892-14-7

LCCN: 90-084154

Cover illustration: Joe Alexander

Printed in the United States of America
Blue Dolphin Press, Inc., Grass Valley, California

9   8   7   6   5   4   3   2

CONTENTS

ABOUT THE AUTHOR

THE AUTHOR IS INFORMED that some readers like to know what the author of a book looks like, so here are a few self-portraits he has drawn for the benefit of readers of this type.

Other items on his resume: Born 1951; Sagittarius. Finished 11th grade and two first-year college courses. No degrees or credentials or qualifications of any sort whatsoever. Major lifelong interest has been art, specifically painting. Makes a living painting signs, portraits, landscapes and mandalas. Hasn't done any airbrushed vans, though he'd love to see some "Garden of Eden" murals on vans instead of all these silly morbid monster things. Not married. No kids. Major goal in life is to fulfill the prophecy that Van Gogh wrote that, "The painter of the future will be a colorist such as has never been seen before." Thinks nobody has been able to fulfill it properly yet because all the painters pollute their sense of color with cooked food, and that the raw food diet is the way to liberate a painter's sense of color so he or she can DO IT!

Joe Alexander

AUTHOR'S DEDICATION

WHEN I LIVED IN TORONTO, I was friends for a while, with an Indian woman (that's a native Canadian red Indian, not an East Indian) who thought I was pretty dumb, and could be I gave her some reasons to think so! Then one day she read one of my booklets on fruitarianism and raw food diet. "I didn't know you had so much common sense!" she said, and said that next time she went shopping she was going to stock up on fruit.

So this book is dedicated to all the people who love nature and love common sense, in the hope that it may help some of them to enjoy more of both. And special thanks and dedications to the publisher, Paul Clemens, for pushing me to write it and having probably more faith in the value of what I say here than I have myself.

This is the diet that *really* works. People who experience raw food diet tend to see it as the key to regaining Paradise on Earth. However, we're all affected by conditions around us, so nobody can go completely back to Paradise until everybody wants to. The more people on the trip, the faster and further we can all go. So please consider coming along.

PUBLISHER'S PREFACE

B LUE DOLPHIN ATTEMPTS TO PUBLISH BOOKS that will help people become better people. We do not expect that everyone who reads this book will take up a strictly raw food diet. We do know, however, that this material will challenge you to become more aware of what you eat . . . and help you explore who and what you are as a human being on this earth.

We originally published this material in a much abbreviated form in 1982. We found that a number of people who were already quite ill were attracted to a raw food diet. We therefore want to make it clear that a raw food diet alone may not automatically heal someone who is sick. While everything you do is your own responsibility, the author's real hope is that young, healthy people will begin to eat more naturally . . . from Mother Nature's kitchen . . . and develop "sound minds in sound bodies."

Modern research shows that the physical body will tend to heal itself when all the factors involved in health are in alignment. Dis-ease is insidious. It often appears in the "unconscious" thought forms of the etheric body of an individual and manifests on the physical only after it has been hosted by a complicated imbalance of psychological and emotional confusions, pressures and rigidities. We can only urge each individual to deal with all levels of his or her own life, and to seek help from others as appropriate.

We hope you will find Joe's book readable, entertaining, and informative. While Joe's writing is alternately witty, serious, historical, and personal, his real goal is to help people tap a reservoir of raw energy at the core of our being . . . and thus take another step into the unknown on our journey of discovering who we really are.

INTRODUCTION

OUR HIGHLY TECHNOLOGICAL SOCIETY has processed, refined and tampered with food to the point where most products in a grocery cart today are unrecognizable as to their source. Boxes of sugared and colored shapes called cereals and pastas and soda pop full of unknown chemicals infiltrate our cupboards. Cans and packages of drugged meat also fill the rows. Our unfounded trust in the innocuous nature and nutritive value of these products needs to be educated. The truth needs to be spread that these chemicals added to our food and the stripping away of our nutrients is detrimental to our health and well-being.

Food should be regarded as medicine with a complex pharmacology, and this is made more complicated by the addition of thousands of chemicals into our food, making foods essentially drugs with certain side effects. Perhaps too, our prevalent problem of obesity is partially related to craving for nutrients (known and those as yet undiscovered) that have been processed out of our food.

America's material affluence has led to a nation that is overfed but undernourished. A diet based on meat and very little fresh raw food is deficient in many nutrients, including the very important essential fatty acids, linoleic and linolenic acids, found only in plant sources (seeds, nuts, avocadoes, beans, grains, etc.). These fats, which we must have in our diets as we cannot synthesize them ourselves, are precursors of an important class of substances called prostaglandins. Prostaglandins are essentially modulators of hormone activity. They have been found to be important in various disorders as high blood pressure, ulcers, asthma, menstrual cramps and toxemia of pregnancy. These fats may be chemically altered by cooking and processing, thus their sources should be eaten fresh and raw.

On the other hand, the typical American diet is sickeningly rich in saturated animal fat and overabundant in protein. This high saturated fat and high protein diet has been correlated with higher rates of cancer and heart disease, major killers in our society. This type of diet is also lacking in fiber. Fiber may be defined as that part of food that passes undigested into the colon (large intestine). Low fiber diets are thought to have a role in appendicitis, diverticular disease, cancer of the colon, constipation, hemorrhoids, varicose veins, diabetes and heart disease. Popular foods such as hamburgers, pizzas, cheese, fried chicken and hot dogs are low in fiber and high in saturated fat and protein.

Hopefully this short introduction has interested you in improving your diet. My good friend, Joe Alexander, certainly is an inspiration to eating better to feel better. He radiates good vibrations and has more energy than anyone I know.

Best wishes,
Terri Su, M.D.

1 INTRODUCTION TO RAW FOODISM

THERE ARE DOZENS and hundreds and thousands of diets, diet books and diet experts in the world today. Most people live on an omnivorous diet—that is, anything that is possible to chew up and swallow and live long enough to tell about it, they will eat. But for one reason or another, many people have decided to adopt some restrictions.

Sometimes the reason is one's alignment with a religious tradition. For instance, some people won't drink wine or eat pork, or they won't eat meat on Fridays, or they eat unleavened bread on certain holidays. There is little health value in following these customs, but many people do it anyway because they feel there's something virtuous or holy about following some ancient tradition.

Some people don't want to kill animals for food, thinking it unjustified cruelty; so they become vegetarians and won't eat any meat.

Some people hope to gain better health through some dietary restriction; one wants to lose weight, or overcome disease or prevent disease, or feel one's best. When people want to go about changing their diet to become healthier, there are two basic approaches to follow in deciding what changes to make. The first is the approach of most doctors, dieticians, diet authors and so forth, and that is the "one baby-step forward at a time" approach. That is, they take the average, common, omnivorous junk food diet as the standard of what is "normal"—not for any particularly good reason, they just figure that since millions of people manage to survive on it, it must be good, and in fact they think it may be dangerous to deviate much from it—and then try to figure out what is the SMALLEST change we can make that will give us some little bit of benefit. For instance, you may be a little better off if you sweeten your pies with honey instead of sugar. Or you may reduce your risk of heart attack by eating lean beef instead of the fattier sorts. Or you may get less constipated by eating brown bread instead of white.

The other way is the "quantum leap" approach. This approach starts off with the common-sense premise that what is most NATURAL for us is likely to be best for our health! So following this approach, we say, never mind what we have gotten used to, but let's consider, if we didn't have thousands of generations of gradually more and more unnatural dietary habits behind us now determining what we eat, what would our natural diet be like? The logical conclusion seems to be that the natural diet would consist of foods we could eat and enjoy—whole, unprocessed and uncooked, just the way Nature gives them to us.

An interesting fact to note is that the most idealistic emotional feelings tend to lead people to feel that a diet of raw fruits, nuts and vegetables is "lightest, purest and most beautiful," while unprejudiced reasoning leads us to the conclusion that these things must be our natural diet because they are the foods we are attracted to and enjoy in their raw, natural state. The most pure-hearted intuition and the most thoroughly rational science always lead to the same point.

The greatest value of the raw food diet is its transformative value. To a great extent, when you take up the raw food diet, you become a new and different and better person. You don't just stay the same old person, only a little healthier. You become, to a great extent, a new being with new interests, a new philosophy and outlook on life, new goals and desires. You become more of your essence, your true and natural self. You become a person who is more a part of the one great life of Nature and less of the confused human world. You become less "of the World" and more "of the Earth."

Such transformations of course are impossible to imagine before you have experienced them. So the raw food diet doesn't so much "improve you" as "replace you" with somebody better! One of the most common statements of people who take up raw food diet in middle age or later, is that they now feel younger than they did even as teenagers. And yet at the same time they feel possessors of an ancient and ageless and eternal wisdom. The spirit is old and wise, and fresh and young at the same time.

Raw foodists get new insight into how much better (than we commonly imagine) life can and should be, how Nature intended it to be. The common little miseries of life, such as frequent colds and flu, indigestions, chapping of the hands and lips in cold weather, bad breath, sluggishness and depression, disappear, and become seen as not natural and normal parts of life at all, but indications of an unbalanced and unhealthy, chronically poisoned condition.

Unfortunately most of us who take up the raw food diet in our adult years have already been badly damaged by our preceding years and generations of unnatural living. Most of us already have decayed teeth and other deformities. But we do the best we can, and hope that by writing books and spreading this knowledge we can influence a widespread return to more natural living so that future generations do not have to suffer as we have. And of course there is the matter of reincarnation: we want to propagate knowledge that can help make this world a better place to be reborn into! That is one reason why I am trying to spread the knowledge and practice of a raw food diet. If reincarnation is true and I am to be reborn into this world, I want this knowledge widely available so I can rediscover it again!

Certain studies by eminent scientists have shown that unnatural diet in childhood leads to certain irreversible physical deformities. They studied primitive peoples living on natural food and then noted the changes in succeeding generations as they took up "civilized" diets including sugar, white flour, liquor and so forth. Most noticeable was a narrowing of the structure of the facial bones with teeth developing poorly. It then becomes logical to speculate that other bone structures, such as the pelvis, may also develop abnormally on unnatural food, and this may be one of the main reasons that civilized women often have such a difficult time in childbirth. And if the body cannot develop normally, how can we expect the mind to? As Arnold Ehret wrote, once you have taken a few steps on the road back to Paradise Health, you see that modern man is not at all a highly intelligent and advanced creature, but a degenerated shadow of what he ought to be.

I have read in farmers' magazines, that if you want your hogs to fatten up quickly, feed them boiled potatoes, not raw; that if you want your cattle to gain weight, cook their grain; don't feed it to them raw. The huge American overweight problem is probably due to the unnatural eating of cooked foods, rather than any specific types of "fattening" foods.

Why does raw food provide such better nourishment, such superior vitalizing and health-giving qualities, than cooked food? Well, we can look at it from two angles, the material and the immaterial. On the one hand cooking destroys the natural chemical composition of the food. The vitamins are altered and destroyed, the proteins are scrambled, the enzymes are torn to pieces. Even simple mixtures of just a few inorganic elements can often be totally changed in character through cooking over a Bunsen burner. What then of foodstuffs, composed of thousands of the most complex organic chemicals poised in fragile balance?

Taking it from the immaterial angle, the great harm of cooking is that it destroys or drives off the life-force in the food. Just look at how strong and alive a fresh raw carrot looks, and compare that to the limp and decaying appearance of a cooked carrot. Some people are able to dowse the life-force in foods via a pendulum. The wider the circle the pendulum swings in, the greater the life-force. They find that the pendulum indicates much greater life-force in raw foods, as our common sense would expect.

But the most convincing test is that of your own experience. You can make a comparison between a meal of raw vegetables, and a meal of the same types of vegetables cooked. The raw vegetables leave you feeling light, fresh and alert, whereas the same vegetables cooked will make you feel lethargic and sluggish. It is common experience, how one feels lazy, dull and sluggish for hours after a big meal, such as Thanksgiving dinner. But meals of raw food don't produce such lethargy and dullness. Vegetarians don't believe in killing for food, but too often they kill their food by cooking it!

Raw food diet is a sort of rational and healthy austerity. It is the sort of discipline that makes you more free. For example, a skilled draftsman and painter is free to make pictures that look like anything he or she desires to create. The unskilled person is free only to fool around and make childish-looking pictures. The raw food diet is a healthy discipline that frees you to be more creative, work harder and think more clearly. It also makes you more free to enjoy the beauties and wonders of the natural world.

There is a popular saying, "You are what you eat." Well, this is a partial truth. There are many, many factors that go into making up just what and who you are. Food is one of them, and one of no small importance. Diet has much to do with the health of the body and much to do with the basic attitude of the mind, whether it is aspiring, searching for truth and growth, or just wants to stay stuck in the same old rut. Many factors go to make up what we are, and since food is one of considerable importance, I am writing this book to tell what I have learned of the food factor.

2 HISTORY OF RAW FOODISM

O BVIOUSLY RAW FOOD must have constituted the original diet of the first primitive human beings. Then of course at some point far back in prehistory, somebody invented fire, and then somebody else discovered that if a chunk of meat or a root or other such foodstuffs were heated over the fire, they gave off tantalizingly delicious smells, and they become softer and easier to eat, and such food tasted especially good on those cold winter days, and then they discovered that these cooked foods could be combined with each other and with various fragrant and tasty herbs and spices to make delicious stews and soups, and pretty soon everyone was cooking all their food whenever they could. And so the history of raw foodism is the history of the rediscovery of the superior health-giving benefits of a natural diet rather than an artificially-altered one.

The pleasures of cooked food come at a heavy price in health and reduced awareness. Some people are coming to feel that price is too high, and returning to natural diet. In every age and every country there seem to be a few people with extraordinary common sense, an extraordinary ability to reason clearly and see through to the heart of important matters, rather than just drift along with the conventional ideas of the time. So probably a few such people have always, through a combination of common sense and experience, known of the value of a raw food diet.

Now if you are a little bit familiar with statistical techniques of mathematics, you will know that if you measure a large number of people for quantitative determination of any particular quality and plot the results in the form of a graph, you will always get a pattern roughly like this and known as a bell curve:

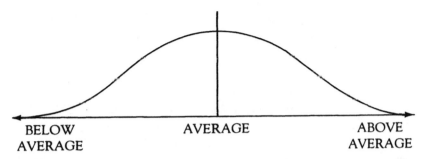

BELOW AVERAGE   AVERAGE   ABOVE AVERAGE

That is, the vast majority will always fall somewhere close to the average, while a small number will find their places at either extreme, whether above or below average. This pattern will apply to measurements of any quality, whether it is height, weight, I.Q., running speed, annual income, or what-have-you. Therefore in this field of health and diet, it naturally follows that most people will adhere to an average, or mediocre diet, neither very superior nor very inferior. Furthermore, it naturally follows that of the hundreds and thousands of doctors, dieticians, nutritionists, diet experts and authors on diet, the vast majority will believe in and advocate a diet of average, or mediocre, health-giving qualities. And the largest, most well-attended and popular schools of medicine, diet and nutrition, will teach mediocre ideas: neither very intelligent nor very foolish. Were they to teach and advocate ideas very much different from what the average person is prepared to accept and believe in, they would not be able to attract large numbers of students. And people grow up with a certain body of ideas and opinions which tend to then constitute their world-view for the rest of their life, and they will not accept any ideas very much different from those implanted in the mind during childhood and adolescence—a little bit different, perhaps, but not much different. As the I Ching says, a popular leader must advocate a very small change for the better. If a leader attempts to advocate a large change, very much for the better, only a tiny minority will be prepared to accept such an idea, and the leader will have only a tiny following and be considered an extremist.

Now the popular press and mass media always promote the silly notion that whatever very large numbers of people do and believe in, must be the truth and the intelligent thing. They always promote the notion that anything believed in and done by only a small number of people, is always a crackpot and lunatic-fringe idea. And so you see their mania for "public opinion polls," oblivious to the obvious fact that really intelligent opinions will only be held by a very few people. This also accounts for the two sorts of people who end up in trouble with the law and in jail. The job of lawmakers is to define average standards of ethical behavior, and the job of the police and courts is to enforce such average, or mediocre, standards of behavior. Those whose behavior is significantly inferior or superior to these mediocre standards usually end up in trouble with the law and in jail. Their actions threaten the inertia of society, which does not want to change much for either the better or worse, though slight changes for the worse are always much more acceptable than slight changes for the better. It's always easier to drift down than climb up.

So any health and diet idea which is much different from the average, has the chance of being either far inferior or far superior to the average. I leave it to you to judge whether raw food diet is superior or inferior.

The truth of what I am saying can be readily seen, by the fact that most people who are attracted to raw foodism don't actually do it because it would make them too different from other people. Their husband or wife or friends or someone else wouldn't go for it. They think they wouldn't be able to enjoy social occasions, eating with their friends and relatives, anymore. Well, it's a choice we have to make sometimes. Are we going to stick with what we believe in and try to bring others up, or let others drag us down?

NOW THE EARLIEST DOCUMENT that I know of that advocates a raw food diet, has been translated in two versions, one by Professor Edmond Bordeaux Szekely and called *The Essene Gospel of Peace*, and the other by Dr. Johnny Lovewisdom and called *The Healing*

God Spell of St. John. The book contains a story of a certain noteworthy healer who is supposed to have lived some 2,000 years ago, and in Prof. Szekely's version the healer is Jesus, and in Dr. Lovewisdom's he is John the Baptist. This healer successfully cured people of all sorts of diseases by instructing them to fast one day for each year of their life, while taking enemas through a gourd to wash out their lower intestines. After their fast he would instruct them to follow a simple vegetarian diet of raw fruits and vegetables plus a kind of bread, known today as Essene Bread, and consisting of whole wheat grains soaked and allowed to begin sprouting, then ground to paste and spread into thin cakes on flat stones and placed in the sunlight to bake. And the people who followed his instructions would get cured of all their diseases and remain in excellent health until the day they died. And my apologies to any Natural Hygienic readers I may have, who believe that you CURE hams but you REMOVE THE CAUSES of diseases, IF you're smart enough to be a Natural Hygienist!

There are some raw foodists who maintain that the Bible teaches a raw food diet, and the way they make out that this is so, is by pointing out that God's original instructions to Adam and Eve in the *Book of Genesis*, were to eat fruits and herbs, and their lifespans allegedly ran up to several hundred years in those days, some of them living to be as old as Methuselah. Then after the Flood we first find mention of cooking and meat eating (though these raw foodists never explain why, if the antediluvian peoples were following God's instructions to live on a natural diet of fruits and herbs, they became so wicked as to motivate God to instigate the Flood in the first place), and lifespans then began to plummet down down down to threescore and ten and then even later we find that Jesus only lived thirty-three years!

It's an interesting theory but my opinion is that nowhere and never does the Bible plainly and unequivocally advocate a raw food diet. Of course, many writers on raw foodism as well as many other subjects, always bend over backwards trying to somehow prove that the Bible supports their theories. This is on account of this cultural thought form that has been dunned into our brains over and over again all our lives like hammering in a railroad spike, that "the Bible is the Word of God," "All Truths are in the Bible," "The Bible is the Ultimate Infallible Authority" etc. etc. etc., so that many people imagine that if only they can prove that the Bible agrees with them, they have won their case. Actually I have found the Bible to be one of the least helpful books in getting at the truth about health and diet. Maybe, just maybe, it has a few little helpful hints here and there but in any case they are so subtle that they might as well not be there at all. And then of course in the New Testament, Jesus throws out the famous red herring "not by what goes down your throat but by what comes out of your heart that you are defiled" which makes many religious types feel smugly justified in eating any sort of junk and not trying to improve their diet at all. In any case, if someone wanted a good book on health and diet to read, I can think of dozens of good authors whose books would be far more worthwhile reading than the Bible.

In the middle ages we find the story of Luigi Cornaro, who lived high in his younger years, feasting and partying and drinking, and then as he got into middle age he became very ill. He was a man of extraordinary powers of reasoning, and he figured that since all the feasting and drinking had made him sick, if he did the exact opposite and ate and drank very little, he ought then to get well. So he cut his rations down to only twelve ounces of food and fourteen ounces of wine per day, with the result that he completely regained his health and enjoyed a very vigorous life until his death at age 98. Now he was not eating only raw food, he was eating meat and bread and soup and egg yolks, besides the wine, but his story illustrates the point that raw foodists are always stressing, that diseases are primarily caused by the foul wastes of superfluous food, cluttering up the body.

This principle has also been known for thousands of years by the Far Eastern Yogis of India who have not only valued fasting as an excellent measure for purification of the body, but also developed sophisticated practices of hatha yoga to mechanically clean wastes from the system. For instance they would bit by bit swallow a long strip of soft cotton cloth which would absorb excessive mucus that was lining the inside of the stomach and digestive tract, and then draw this cloth back out through the mouth, thus removing these encumbrances from the body. Likewise they developed similarly sophisticated methods to clean out the respiratory passages and lower intestines, and even today if you go to Connaught Circus in Delhi, you will be accosted by bright-eyed young men armed with precision steel instruments, offering to clean the excessive dirty wax from your ears!

And in his book *Autobiography of a Yogi*, Paramahansa Yogananda mentions that he once met a yogi who had maintained a fruitarian diet for the past nine years, and the tone of the writing indicated that the author admired and felt there was virtue in such a regimen.

Now the advances of modern technological civilization have poisoned every square inch of the world and they have created filth, misery, poverty, death and suffering on such a grand scale as has never been seen before, but one of the happy results of this technological advancement has been the publication and mass worldwide distribution of millions of copies of inexpensive paperback books, a few of them actually containing useful information. Thus nowadays, because archaic notions of "freedom of the press" and "freedom of speech" have still not been entirely eradicated by the U.S. and other governments, health-and-truth seekers all around the world are able to read about and benefit from the knowledge and experiences of others of like mind. So nowadays, millions of people have been exposed to the concept of a natural raw food diet, which they probably wouldn't have thought of themselves. And as a few of them have actually taken it up, there are nowadays dozens and maybe even hundreds of new books and magazine articles published every year, advocating the natural raw-food diet, so that I no longer feel any particular distinguishment in being a raw foodist author; they are coming out of the woodwork from all sides, as we enter the post-Harmonic Convergence era of world post-history!

Backtracking a little, we find in the nineteenth century, the work of such pioneering physicians as Russell Trall, John Tilden and Sylvestor Graham forming the foundations of Natural Hygiene and the modern health-food movement.

Now at the root of the theory of natural hygiene lies the simple but utterly profound concept, revolutionary in its vast implications to the unipolar and thus lopsided hypotheses which constitutes the orthodox contemporary medical postulates, that the predominant cause of most of the pathological conditions to which the physical human vehicle is commonly prone and which are generally classified as being states of dis-ease, lies not in the externally-originating invasion of the human body by inimical swarming hosts of detrimental microbe, demons, evil spirits or other such exotic agents of causation, but in the superfluous internal production of both physically and chemically encumbering wastes and toxin, all non-utilitarian by-products of the customary metabolism, and which tend to internally accumulate in such abnormally great quantities and concentrations as to finally constitute a positively debilitating influence, and which accumulation most readily and nearly exclusively occurs when the individuals' habitual consumption of comestibles consists primarily of foodstuffs manufactured and/or artificially subject to severe alteration so that such ingesta present the human digestive secretions with the daily and continual challenge of attempting effectively to deal with altogether unnatural substances and compounds which the adaptations of previous evolution and the designing hand of the agents of vital organic creation have not adequately prepared the human gastro-intestinal family of internal organs to shoulder the unwonted burden for the proper and efficient processing of. There you have Natural Hygiene defined in a one-sentence nutshell!

So natural hygiene recommends that while ill and without appetite, the best thing for us to do is fast. By fasting, they mean to refrain from all food except water. People talk about "juice fasting" and "fruit fasting," but I agree that this confuses the meaning of the word "to fast," and it would be best to reserve the word "fasting" for those times when we go without any nourishment except water.

Ramakrishna said that some people when they fast neither eat nor drink anything at all; some people drink water when they fast, then some people also eat fruit when they fast, and then again some people also eat vegetables when they fast; and some people when they fast also eat bread and rice, and some people also eat chicken and fish when they fast, and then again, some people also eat beef and pork when they fast!

It's like Bhagwan Shree Rajneesh's joke: Two old Jews were talking and one says, "I've got a riddle! What's green, hangs on the wall, and whistles?"

"I give up," said the other. "What is it?"

"A red herring!"

"But you said it was green!"

"So, you can paint it green."

"But you said it hangs on the wall!"

"So you can nail it to the wall."

"But you said it whistles!"

"So, it doesn't whistle."

Nothing is left of the original proposition.

So from here on when I talk about fasting in this book, I refer to going with no food, only water.

So natural hygiene says that when we are sick, we lose our appetite and desire for food, and this means we would do well to follow the urge of nature and refrain from eating. For when we go without eating, we relieve our system of the burden of processing and ingesting new food, so that it can turn all energies into the job of eliminating the wastes accumulated from previous unnatural and over-eating, which are causing us to feel ill in the first place. Drugs suppress the symptoms of disease, interfere with the body's self-cleansing efforts and don't remove the causes of the disease; thus the drug-taker is likely to become sick again soon, and possibly develop very serious diseases later in life as a result of never allowing him-or-her self to undergo a thorough house-cleaning.

Further, natural hygiene says we can avoid accumulating further causes of diseases by eating only natural food and following the common-sense rule of not eating when we're not hungry.

Healers who practice natural hygienic principles seem to almost routinely enjoy success in helping their patients overcome all sorts of conditions which the orthodox medical practitioners have found to be "incurable." However, it is good to stress the point that there is no good reason to wait until one has an "incurable" disease before taking up a natural hygienic way of life, because even people with no outright symptoms of disease will feel marvelously better when they get their bodies cleaned up and adhere to a natural diet. This provides the answer to a certain class of fools who enjoy repeating the idea that health nuts are depriving themselves of great pleasures, that even if they are healthy and live long, their lives are dull and boring. The truth is this. First of all the raw foodist health nut enjoys the rich variety of subtle flavors in natural foods, rather than the grossly over-refined and concentrated imbalanced flavors of junk foods, which are always grossly overloaded in one of three ways: sickeningly sweet from white sugar, too salty, or too much hot spice. Then the raw foodist health nut also enjoys the pleasure of peace and cleanliness within the body, and the ultimate spiritual pleasure of oneness with nature. There's no pleasure greater than feeling comfortable in your own body. People seek for luxurious houses and soft furniture trying in vain to make up for the discomfort caused by junk food eating. The raw foodist would enjoy a higher standard of living in a little hut than a junk food eater could in a palace. And raw foodism aids greatly in developing the spiritual maturity necessary for truly worthwhile achievements in life.

The noted 19th-century poet Shelley was one of the first natural-diet advocates, who clearly saw the connection between unnatural diet and the great problems of society such as crime, poverty and injustice and corrupt governments. In his "Introduction to Queen Mab" he notes how natural food makes us desire a life based on subsistence, on a close and loving relationship with the land; we feel it a privilege and honor and deep pleasure to work on the land for our subsistence. On unnatural food, our spiritual connection with the land is disturbed and we come to desire a life based on commerce and consumption of exotic goods from far away. And with commerce as the basis of life, rather than subsistence, there develops the stratification of society into rich and poor classes which is the basis for crime, injustice and corrupt governments. Were it universally adopted, natural diet would make everyone desire to work a small area of land for their subsistence and thus eliminate the major political and economic problems at one fell swoop.

Now the interesting thing about the most effective modern discoveries regarding treatment of disease and maintenance of health, is that they are essentially identical to the procedures described in the 2,000 year old *Essene Gospel* or *Healing God Spell*. Thus we have here a true science, which has discovered the real nature and requirements of the human body, which has not significantly changed over the centuries. Medical fads and fashions come and go; thousands of new drugs are put on the market every year and thousands more taken off; but inner cleanliness and natural diet remain ever and always the most reliable ways to prevent and eliminate most diseases as well as maintain the best possible health.

The best books on health are still not generally available in major bookstores and libraries, and especially not in university libraries, although a notable exception, *Fit For Life*, an excellent book on Natural Hygiene, has become a national bestseller. So you often have to poke around a little in out-of-the-way places to get the best information which can help you to the best of health. Remember, it says that the gates to destruction are plenty wide enough for everyone to drive through in air-conditioned Greyhound buses lined up ten abreast, but the gates to truth are very low and narrow and you have to squeeze through one at a time and you can't even take your backpack. It says this in the Bible. See, I like to quote the Scriptures too, if it suits my purposes.

So now in the next chapter I want to briefly describe and summarize the teachings of some of the more distinguished 20th century authors and proponents of raw food diets. This should provide readers a nice sort of bird's-eye view of the contemporary raw foodist scene and the variety of points of view within it.

SOME NOTABLE RAW FOODISTS AND THEIR TEACHINGS

3

PROFESSOR ARNOLD EHRET WAS the first raw foodist writer whose books I read, the one who got me interested in the whole subject, and I still think that, with his forceful descriptions of the heightened pleasures of life on natural diet, he is still the most inspiring, the most likely to give the reader the charge of enthusiasm needed to burn one's bridges and actually do it! Ehret's writings are like science and poetry rolled into one, and I still think he has given the clearest, most understandable description of the process whereby the body can become burdened with toxins and excessive mucus, and what must be done to clean these out, and what symptoms a person is likely to go through during such a cleansing process.

Ehret's two major books are *Rational Fasting* and *Mucusless Diet Healing System*, and his publisher has organized some of his shorter essays into booklets such as *Thus Speaketh the Stomach*, *The Definite Cure of Chronic Constipation*, and *Roads to Health and Happiness*.

Many people criticize Prof. Ehret for being such an extremist and fanatic about a fruitarian diet, and the reason he was a fanatic about it was that it was the only thing that was finally able to save

26

his life when he was dying from a kidney problem called Bright's disease. He first tried all medical treatments for his problem that were available in Europe at the time, which was early in the 1900s. His condition continued to worsen under these treatments and finally his physicians pronounced him incurable. He then turned to the various naturopathic treatments that were available, with the result of some relief and a renewed desire to live, but never complete healing. Studying all he could about health and diet, he finally took matters into his own hands and undertook a series of fasts with fruitarian diet, with the result that not only did his kidney problem completely disappear, but he came also to enjoy the best health of his life, a state of vitality and mental clarity so much superior to anything he had ever known before that he called it "Paradise Health." Thus Prof. Ehret is one of the "practical paradisean" writers of the 20th century. These practical paradiseans are people who not only hope, dream, long for and speculate about a future world of great happiness, but have also undertaken determined and serious research to discover the root causes of human problems and miseries, and they have in fact by now discovered all these basic root causes in the fundamental fields of health, psychology, economics and ecology. These are the foundations of our lives, upon which the whole human cultural superstructure rests. And so the causes and solutions to all the major human miseries are now known. Any statements you may hear that our great problems, such as disease, alienation, poverty, pollution etc. are very complicated and nobody really knows how to solve them, merely show the speaker's ignorance. Solutions to all major human problems and miseries have been found. It just needs more people to recognize this and put these solutions into practice.

Professor Ehret's health teachings, in summary, say that the vast majority of conditions of impaired health are due to accumulation of poisons and excessive mucus within the body, which restrict proper functioning both chemically and mechanically. Common disease symptoms such as running nose and clogged sinuses, coughing up of mucus from the lungs, outbreaks on the

skin, discharges in the urine and so forth—are the body's attempts
to excrete superfluous mucus which hinder its proper functioning.
So much has accumulated that the normal channels of waste
elimination can't handle it; so the body mobilizes emergency
avenues. Prof. Ehret believed that the precursor condition to most
diseases is constipation, which allows the body to become
gradually more and more overloaded with waste matters until
finally obvious illness develops.

Now the cause of this constipation is the common diet that
nearly everyone lives on. Our common cooked starchy and high-
protein foods are sticky and gluey; they are difficult for the
digestive system to move along smoothly and efficiently; also,
being cooked into unnatural substances, they are difficult to
digest and remain in the system for an inordinate length of time.
The worst of them are the sticky and gluey dairy products such as
cheese, and the white flour and white rice products which have
been stripped of their natural roughage leaving nothing but pure
starch, i.e., paste. Then also the whole grains, eggs, meats, cooked
beans, and potatoes are also quite heavy, sticky and gluey. So
when such foods are eaten three or more times daily, the body
cannot eliminate the resulting sticky, mucus waste products as fast
as new mucus-forming foods are taken in, so an accumulation of
mucus develops which finally erupts as symptoms of "cold,"
"flu," "tuberculosis" etc.

By contrast, Prof. Ehret advocated a "mucusless diet" of
primarily fruits and green-leaf vegetables. You can easily make a
personal test to see the difference. Take a piece of white bread,
butter it and put on some cheese or egg or meat to make a
sandwich. Chew it up and swallow it. Notice how sticky and gluey
it is, how hard to swallow and how residual slime from it remains
in your mouth. Now take an apple or orange or celery or cabbage
leaves, chew it up and swallow it. Notice how these watery foods
are much easier to swallow and tend to clean out your mouth.
Even a sticky fruit, such as a date, dissolves in water, whereas flour
mixed with water forms paste. Thus when the diet consists mostly
or entirely of these mucusless foods, the fruits and salad vege-

tables, constipation is not encouraged to develop and the body remains free from exorbitant accumulations of internal wastes and thus the common diseases have no opportunity to develop.

It is quite amazing how much waste matter an average healthy person, even a thin one, can carry around without suffering from continual outright symptoms of disease, except for colds and flu several times a year. But even so, these waste matters always depress and devitalize to some extent, and so most so-called healthy individuals who fast and live on mucusless diet enough to thoroughly clean out their system, will be astonished at how much lighter, cleaner and more energetic they come to feel, how their emotions tend to stabilize at a higher tone and their minds work more clearly.

However, Prof. Ehret believed that immediately taking up a natural, uncooked mucusless diet would prove too uncomfortable and even dangerous for most people; the elimination would be too dramatic and drastic, so he worked out a "transition diet" to enable health-seekers to undergo a more gradual and comfortable cleansing period and finally transition to the ideal diet. He rated foods as mucus-forming, mucus-lean, and mucus-less. So the transition diet consists first of mostly mucus-lean foods, with gradually more and more of the mucusless. Mucus-lean foods include sweet potatoes, baked potatoes, whole-grain crackers, nuts and fish. Mucus-forming foods include dairy products, white flour and white rice, breads and porridges of all sorts, eggs, meats and beans. The mucus-less foods are fruits and starchless vegetables.

In addition to the mucus-forming foods, there are many commonly consumed items which, while mucusless, are chemically poisonous; such include refined sugar, salt, coffee, tea, alcohol, soft drinks, tobacco, and all the artificial preservatives, additives and flavorings as well as pesticide residues and now URP's, unique radiolytic products, by-products of food irradiation. It is impossible to avoid all of these, but the person who loves life tries to as best s/he can!

Arshavir Ter Hovannessian, from Iran, is another outstanding raw-foodist writer. His book is entitled, *Raw Eating* and he is founder of a "Raw Vegetarian Society."

In his book he discusses the philosophy of raw eating and tells of his own return to fine health as the result of following this diet. From a sickly, middle-aged man on the conventional diet, only able to work a few hours daily, he took up raw eating and came to feel more vigorous than in his youth, able to run up mountains and work tirelessly all day and late into the night. He advocates a "systemless system" of raw food eating, that is, to eat any sort of raw vegetarian food, in any desired quantities, in any desired combinations, whenever you feel like eating. In other words, use your common sense to restrict your diet to natural foods and then listen to your body. Hovannessian believes that all raw vegetarian foods as created by nature, contain perfect nourishment and we could live on any one such item indefinitely; thus he says there is no need at all to concern oneself with laboratory calculations of calories, vitamins, proteins etc., as all such studies are carried out with denatured foodstuffs on unhealthy people and therefore are misleading and unnecessary where healthy people and a natural diet are concerned. The need and desire for a "science of health and nutrition" arose because we began eating unnaturally and thus making ourselves sick; get back to a natural diet and the problems become solved and the need for such a science vanishes.

Hovannessian writes that after years of recommending transition diets, he now feels the best thing is to go directly into a complete raw food diet. He also does not advocate long fasts, feeling that to do so depresses the body of badly-needed vital nourishment from raw foods, and that when you return to this natural diet the body will accomplish all necessary cleansing without need of prolonged fasting. In the back of his book, Hovannessian prints testimonial letters from readers who have suffered from all manner of ailments and been restored to health through following a raw vegetarian diet. One man felt his return to vigorous health was so miraculous that he exclaimed in his letter to Hovannessian, "You are the Christ!"

Hovannessian publishes, in his book, a photo of his teenaged daughter who has been all her life exclusively a raw eater; he says she has never eaten a bit of cooked food in her life. He says that it is less trouble to raise one hundred raw eating children than one cooked food eater; that the daughter's older brothers, raised on conventional cooked food, were frequently sick, noisy and messy in their play and frequently having unpleasant emotional outbursts and tantrums. By contrast the raw eating daughter, he said, never got sick and played quietly and happily.

Parents of my acquaintance, however, who have tried to raise their kids on natural diet, do not have an easy time of it. For one thing, they don't stick to it all that closely themselves, thus not setting a consistent example. It is possible for adults to follow principles and reason, but small children follow examples. For another thing, they generally don't start until the kids are already several years old and already addicted to the taste of cooked food. Cooked food is the most difficult of all addictions to break, more difficult than cigarettes or liquor or heroin, and especially if you don't want to, which these kids never do want to. So the kids are always demanding cooked food and junk food and are determined to cry, scream and holler until they get it, which seldom takes long because nowadays parents are not firm and consistent with their children, so the kids know very well that if they cry and holler for x number of minutes, the parents will always cave in and give them anything they want. As well, of course nowadays the government is now encouraging Americans to spy on each other and give the police anonymous tips and turn their neighbors in, as did the Nazi government and the government of Soviet Russia. So parents have to be always careful that some nosey and anonymous neighbor is not going to turn them in for Child Abuse and the government take their kids away from them. Some neighbors are so ignorant that they will report people for child abuse if they just try to bring up their kids vegetarian. And of course there is the problem of compulsory vaccinations for the kids to go to school. Anyone who really looks into the issue soon finds that these vaccinations generally do more harm than good, if any good at all. For instance, nobody died of the Swine Flu, but several people died of the

Swine Flu Vaccine. Recently I heard a news report of an outbreak of measles in the schools of Houston, where 90% of the students have been vaccinated for measles! And I was recently reminded of the polio vaccine business. I remember as a child getting first polio shots and then a couple of boosters. Apparently kids were getting polio vaccine and then getting polio nonetheless; so they said you needed a booster shot; then when kids still got polio they said you needed a third booster and then maybe even a fourth. They ignored a doctor who virtually wiped out polio in his state for a while by getting parents to quit feeding their kids so much sugar. Eleanor McBean appears to have researched the vaccination business better than anyone else; she has written *The Poisoned Needle* and a couple of other eye-opening books. But parents who don't believe in vaccination have an awful hard time keeping their kids from compulsory school vaccinations.

And then of course the overwhelming interest of kids is never principles or truth or health, but social life, to get along with and be respected by the other kids. And they will catch all sorts of devilish tormenting from their friends at school if all they bring for lunch is "bunny food." So they want salami sandwiches to look normal to their friends. And then also, parents always tend to react in the worst possible way and lecture the kids on "what's good for you." And of course when the kids get that sort of stuff shoved down their throats, all they want to do is REBEL and eat the worst junk they can find! So it's a very tough situation, this business of trying to raise healthy kids. Hovannessian may have found it easy to raise a child as a raw eater, but I don't know anyone else who says so!

I have this one comment to make on Hovannessian's "systemless system" of eating raw vegetarian foods in any desired combinations, and that is that I think it is really worthwhile to follow the basic Natural Hygienic principles of food combining (to be described later); especially the combination of fruit and seeds is terrible and is likely to cause trouble for anyone. These "trail mixes" of dried fruits and nuts really are an abomination. Of course, if you really listen to your body you will find it doesn't want the bad combinations; it has an instinct for the good combinations.

Dr. *Johnny Lovewisdom* is another very outstanding raw food advocate. His goal in life has been to discover the solution to all human problems and the secret of physical immortality. I once saw a color photo of him in his 60's and he looked like a radiantly happy 35 year old, with a full head of hair and not a trace of gray in his blond hair and beard. It did indeed look like he had found the secret of eternal or at least greatly prolonged youth. I have heard though, that he is crippled, which he says is because of Parathion poisoning earlier in life when he worked in apple orchards in California.

He calls his system the Vitarian way of life. He says that in adolescence, the body begins to wear out because of the undue strain imposed on the digestive system and liver by foods too high in starch and protein, as well as any other poisons entering the system through eating, drinking or breathing. So the body, sensing that its eventual death is inevitable, activates the sexual reproductive system with accompanying sexual desire so that the species may be continued through creation of new bodies, though the individual must eventually die. But Lovewisdom says that by living on the Vitarian diet of "living water" foods, fruits and vegetables containing about 90% of water in their composition, the liver and digestive system are not overburdened with the excess starch and protein of rich foods, thus the body does not gradually decay and wear out; the sexual reproductive system does not reach mature activation and all energy that would have gone to sexual activity is channelled instead into renewal of the body, and development of higher mental and psychic faculties. To be effective for these purposes, such a Vitarian diet must be organic-ally grown with no trace of pesticides or other artificial poisonous chemicals, and the individual must breathe clean air with no trace of air pollution. Lovewisdom himself lives high in the Andes Mountains in Ecuador, on the western slope; apparently the prevailing winds blow from the east and thus fallout and other pollutants are deposited on the eastern slope of the mountains and thus the western slope is the cleanest available spot on the globe, with possible exception of Antarctica, where the climate of course is too cold to grow fruits. Lovewisdom has founded the International University of Natural Living and the Pristine Order of Paradisean Perfection in order to teach others how they may gain eternally youthful life and the highest possible happiness if they will live by the strictest discipline on Earth, compared with which the discipline of military and business life consists of nothing but slipshod, sloppy indulgence of every sort of weakness.

Lovewisdom points out also, that the cultivation of grain, which forms the mainstay of the conventional diet, necessitates the plowing up of soil every year which allows erosion which eventually turns the land into sterile desert, thus grain-eating cultures always leave a trail of destroyed, lifeless land as their legacy; whereas the cultivation of fruit trees for Vitarian diets creates a stable ecosystem as the tree roots bring up nutrients from deep within the subsoil which then become added to the topsoil as mulch when the trees shed their leaves. The raising of cattle, sheep and goats for meat diets likewise leads to serious erosion which eventually leaves the land as desert.

Lovewisdom points out the falsity of technological development as the supposed road to greater happiness, abundance and paradise on earth. People build machines as a substitute for human capacities which have become atrophied as the result of unnatural way of life. Living on cooked grains, we become sluggish and lazy and want to build cars to ride around in. As our mental faculties degenerate, we try to substitute for them with computers. I have heard that some primitive peoples despised literacy; they didn't want to learn to read because "it will make us stupid and unable to remember!" If we were wiser, we would not so much seek for machines to do our work for us, but for more energy and strength so we would enjoy doing our work, and would know more clearly what is worthwhile doing!

Viktoras Kulvinskas is probably the most famous present-day American exponent of raw-food diet, having attained that position through his book, *Survival into the 21st Century*, which has become an all-time New Age classic.

Kulvinskas is especially notable for advocating the use of young sprouted seeds and young grasses as the major item of the diet. He says that these sprouts, being usually less than two weeks old and thus very much in their immature state, thus contain the substance and vibration of extreme youth, and when they are eaten these youthful substances and vibrations are transferred to our bodies, thus helping to rejuvenate and keep them youthful also.

Kulvinskas regards the chlorophyll of wheatgrass and other young grasses as particularly valuable foods at this time, because apparently it stimulates the body's regenerative powers more than any other food and thus provides a certain amount of protection against smog and pollution and even radioactivity. Wheatgrass, in particular, is reported to have some properties which sound miraculous. For instance a tray of growing wheatgrass placed in front of a color TV set is supposed to neutralize the harmful radiations from the screen before they can get to you. And a sprig of live wheatgrass, swished around for a few moments in a glass of tap water, is supposed to neutralize the poisonous fluorides and chlorines which most cities nowadays dump into the drinking water. That's what I've heard; I can't tell you for sure if it's true.

Kulvinskas has also published the writings of many other fasters and raw foodists in the book *Life in the 21st Century*, which he co-edited with Richard Tasca, Jr. He has also helped much to promote community among natural-living advocates through his *New Age Directory*. He is now promoting blue-green algae as a very valuable dietary supplement, also.

Dr. Ann Wigmore is an outstandingly dedicated healer and promoter of natural diets. She is especially notable as the discoverer of the virtues of wheatgrass and probably the first outstanding promoter of sprouts.

Dr. Wigmore is the founder of Hippocrates Health Institute, described by "Cosmopolitan" magazine as the "well-kept secret" of beauty and rejuvenation of many famous movie stars and celebrities. Well, Dr. Wigmore has been shouting her knowledge to the world with all her strength for a long time; she's definitely not trying to keep anything secret. Besides all her work in this country, she has also travelled and taught extensively in India. She has made cancer a particular subject of her research and many people have gained remission of cancer through following the diet promoted at Hippocrates Health Institute, an outstanding case being that of Eydie Mae, author of *How I Conquered Cancer Naturally*, telling how she gained remission of breast cancer and she and her husband found a new and better life through a visit to Dr. Wigmore's Hippocrates Health Institute.

Herbert Shelton was the most outstanding Natural Hygienic writer and practitioner of the 20th century, the great systematizer of the present System of Natural Hygiene. He was the author of numerous books on diet, fasting, exercise and other health-related topics and somehow also found much time to devote to operating a Health School in San Antonio, Texas, for many years. I believe that Shelton's system of Natural Hygiene can be basically and fairly summed up as follows:

—Diseases result from a combination of enervation and toxemia, enervation being a depletion and shortage of the nerve-force, the vital life energy, toxemia being a self-poisoning of the body by the waste products of foods eaten, along with any other poisons taken into the system through unnatural food additives and preservatives and other sources of environmental pollution which find their way into the human body. Enervation can be caused by overwork or any other activity which tends to exhaust one's energy reserves, and one important cause of enervation would be the common over-eating of cooked and unnatural foodstuffs which thus put a continual daily strain on the digestive organs and entire eliminative system, thus creating a vicious circle of toxemic accumulation due to such destructive eating habits leading to enervation which further diminishes the body's capacity to deal with the accumulated toxemia. Therefore diseases can be most effectively eliminated by removing their cause, which involves:

—Fasting, first of all, in order to give the entire digestive system a complete rest, allowing the organs of elimination to get rid of the existing toxemia without being further hindered by addition of more food. By fasting, Shelton means that one takes no food whatsoever, only such water as one feels a thirst for. Shelton observed that people can safely fast for amazingly long times, citing in his books numerous instances of people fasting 40 days and longer, even up around 100 days, depending on their reserves; of course the heavier people tend to have greater stored reserves to live on while fasting, but even thin and emaciated people, Shelton observed, could fast for surprisingly long times and with benefit to their health. Shelton found that, contrary to certain ignorant medical theories, the body does not, when fasting, begin consuming the heart, lungs, brain tissue, etc. at the same rate as other tissues but instead always breaks down and consumes the least vital tissues first, so that a person can fast a very long time without losing any of the vital substance of the heart, brain and other important organs. Shelton made a clear distinction between fasting and starvation, fasting being the period of time when the one who goes without food, lives on the stored reserves in the body and is therefore not lacking for nourishment at all. During the fasting period the body cleans itself out thoroughly, eliminating toxemia and tumors and other such deposits of surplus and harmful material; when this cleansing is finished, a new sense of health, cleanliness and vitality is experienced and a strong, healthy, natural hunger returns. Shelton found that fasters would often lose their hunger after three or four days, and then could go for weeks without the desire for food, the hunger only returning when the toxemia was all cleaned up. When toxemia had been eliminated and health restored by fasting, one could then remain in excellent health and avoid building any new diseases through

—Natural Diet, consisting of those uncooked vegetarian foods which we enjoy eating in their natural state; the fruits, vegetables, seeds and nuts. Apparently there are people who have taken apart the bodies of all sorts of animals and made various comparative measurements of the respective parts, and they reportedly have found that, anatomically, the human body is most akin to the vegetarian animals, having an intestine some 10 to 12 times the length of the body, whereas the meat-eating carnivores like the dogs and cats have intestines only about 3 or 4 times their body length. Also the digestive juices of the meat-eating carnivores are said to contain much more hydrochloric acid than human digestive juices; the human digestive secretions are apparently more akin to those of the vegetarian animals.

Also they say that the meat-eating animals drink water by lapping it up with the tongue, whereas the vegetarian animals drink water by suction. Humans drink water by suction. Also the meat-eating carnivores have sharp teeth for stabbing their prey to death and ripping the flesh from the bones whereas the vegetarian animals have flatter teeth for crushing and grinding and lack the long sharp fangs of the cat and dog types. Among humans, only the immediate family and first cousins of Dracula have carnivore-type fangs.

Likewise, the human fingers have broad flat nails, suitable for peeling bananas and oranges but not really much good for inflicting fatal wounds such as the claws of lions, tigers, bears, wolves, etc. Likewise, say the Vegetarian advocates, when we come across a dying animal on the road, bleeding to death and moaning piteously while it jerks in convulsive tremors, our reaction is likely to be one of revulsion or sadness, whereas if we were natural carnivores, such a sight ought to immediately make us feel delightfully hungry! In one of Ian Fleming's James Bond novels, he created the incident where Bond's enemy attempted to assassinate Bond by the device of leaving in his hotel room, a large basket full of ripe and luscious fruits, each fruit injected with enough cyanide to wipe out a jumbo-jet full of people. Fleming portrayed this device as extremely clever and well-thought-out because nothing was likely to so tempt a hungry man as to immediately grab it up and take a big bite, without pausing to carefully consider the possible consequences, as a ripe and juicy nectarine. Consider Bond's probable reaction if his enemy had left a dead but still warm and bleeding rabbit in the basket instead of ripe fruits! Humans generally seem to enjoy meat more, the less it resembles the actual animal that it came from. Many people feel sick at the idea of eating a fish which still has the head attached with the eye staring out at them; they at least want the head cut off before they will eat the fish. And consider how popular such items as hot dogs, salami slices, bacon strips, sausage, hamburgers and fish sticks are, which bear no resemblance at all to the living animal. And even most regular meat eaters feel revolted at the idea of eating certain "unusual" organs of the animal, such as the brains, lungs, heart, drinking the blood, and so forth; whereas if we were natural carnivores it would seem we would have an instinctive relish for such items. We seem to only be able to stand eating meat when we have grown habituated and accustomed to it, and then the idea of eating another kind of meat distresses us until we get habituated to it; for instance most meat eaters feel quite revolted at the idea of eating octopus, squid, snails, dog, grasshoppers, grubs, and so forth. By contrast, when we hear of some sort of tropical fruit that we have never eaten before, immediately we desire to try it; there is no resistance as in the case of unaccustomed meats, but a positive eagerness to try it.

—Therefore, Natural Hygiene says that the natural human diet is Vegetarian, and of course it is most natural and therefore most healthful when it is uncooked. And natural foods are best eaten in cetain compatible combinations which make for ease of digestion, viz:

—Fruits must not be combined with vegetables, nuts or seeds. An exception is the avocado, which may be combined with vegetables, seeds, nuts, or citrus fruits.

—Melons must not be combined with any other foods whatsoever; not even with other sorts of sweet juicy fruits.

—Vegetables may be combined with nuts and seeds.

—Water is the only fluid one should ever drink. One must never drink water less than ½ an hour before nor less than 2 hours after a meal.

Best of all are Mono Meals of only one type of food.

In its internal consistency of logic, Herbert Shelton's System of Natural Hygiene is a great work of art, like a universe unto itself. It appears to contain a complete and perfect structure for optimum quality of life, insofar as the physical dimension is concerned. Those who can appreciate the beauty of a logically consistent intellectual structure will find great pleasure in studying Natural Hygiene.

John Tobe was another well-known and influential promoter of raw food diets; in fact he sometimes referred to himself as the world's foremost promoter of a raw food diet. He had his headquarters in St. Catharines, Ontario, Canada, where he published his many books as well as a monthly magazine called the "Provoker." He believed in raw vegetables as the most valuable of all foods, and promoted raw fruits, seeds and nuts as very desirable foods also. Contrary to most raw foodists who are fanatic vegetarians, Tobe would even sometimes speak well of raw milk, eggs, fish and meat. All right then, this provides a good can of worms to open up right now; what about raw milk, eggs, fish and meat?

Milk is usually condemned by raw foodists as a food suitable only for infants and then only for the specific species; i.e., cow's milk should only be drunk by calves, goat's milk by kids, and human babies should only have human milk. It is certainly logical, but even so, I have heard of research that shows that cow's milk only becomes harmful when it is pasteurized and homogenized; apparently the pasteurization turns the cholesterol into a harmful sort of unnatural form and the homogenization fouls up the butterfat particles so that they contribute to hardening of the arteries. Some people have an allergy to milk, they don't have the enzyme to digest it, so of course obviously they shouldn't drink it.

I have heard of an African tribe which lives on nothing but raw milk and raw blood; they keep cattle which they both milk and bleed. And I hear that these people are marvellously healthy on such a diet, having none of the colon diseases which doctors now would expect people to develop on such a diet, lacking in vegetable fibers. Many people would feel revolted at the idea of drinking fresh raw blood, but you have to admit it is more humane to bleed a cow for a couple pints of blood now and then, than to kill it for hamburger!

In an article in the "Toronto Inner Life" magazine in April 1981, Drs. J.J. and N. Hajek wrote, "It is difficult to imagine a more unhealthy regimen than an almost total meat diet. Yet native Eskimos who subsisted on raw meat remained healthy. But when they learned to heat it in our fashion, within 20 years symptoms of degenerative diseases were observed. Similar results were reported with other tribes in different parts of the world when they changed their diet of raw, unrefined foods to cooked, refined ones."

In his autobiography *Seeker of Visions*, Lame Deer, a Sioux Indian, wrote that in the old days when the hunters killed a buffalo, they would cut its belly open so that its intestines would come spilling out and one man would take hold of one end of the intestine and the other would take the other end, and they would eat until they met in the middle. And he said, that that was real eating; that the modern civilized foods the Indians have to eat nowadays just haven't got the power found in such natural foods.

In his book *Food is Your Best Medicine*, Henry Bieler, M.D., tells the story of an Arctic explorer who found that his pack of dried, canned and packaged provisions would be too heavy to carry on his long journeys over the ice. He thought to himself, if the Eskimos could live on raw fish and seal meat that they catch up here, why can't I? So he tried it, and found that for the first few days he was rather revolted by eating raw fish, but he soon learned to enjoy it immensely and found that he felt marvelously strong and healthy on this diet. Later on he brought other young men up to the Arctic and got them on his raw-fish diet. At first, they also felt revolted at it and would sometimes vomit up their raw fish, but after a couple of weeks they all grew to enjoy it, and also felt wonderfully vigorous and healthy on this diet.

Contrast this with what Arshavir Ter Hovannessian said in his book, that certain Asian countries used to execute their condemned prisoners by giving them nothing but cooked meat to eat, and they usually died within thirty days. This of course suggests the answer to those who are seeking the most humane method of execution in this country. You know, it used to be that all the states would hang their condemned prisoners, but then around the turn of the century, the new technology of electricity became all the rage, so the executioners wanted to play with this new technology so they built electric chairs and sold the idea to many of the states on the grounds that it was more fun to be electrocuted to death than hanged. Then a couple decades later the slogan became "better living through chemistry" and the executioners wanted to play with this new technology also, so they built poison-gas chambers and got some of the states to switch to those, again on the grounds that it would be more enjoyable to die in a gas chamber than by the older methods. And of course nowadays the "medical marvels" of heart transplants, mechanical kidneys, IV feeding and so forth, make banner headlines and so naturally the executioners want a slice of this good PR too, so they have now got some of the states to kill their condemned prisoners by strapping them down like a laboratory rat while a smiling young man in a clean white coat pumps a massive lethal dose of sodium pentothal into their veins. And again, of course, they say that it is much more pleasant to die this way, than by the former methods. But Hovannessian's statement should be implemented immediately as the most humane method of execution of all. Feed them steaks and fried chicken until they die of the pleasure!

I recently talked on the phone to a naturopathic doctor in New York who has done considerable research into raw meat. He told me that there is a doctor in France who is having great success healing cancer and all sorts of other degenerative diseases. He said that the way he does it, is to sit his patients down twice a day at a table loaded with raw goodies, raw fruits, raw vegetables, raw seeds and nuts, raw meat, etc., and then has them pick out whichever sort of food they desire and make their entire meal out of it, and eat as much as they want, BUT ONLY ONE ITEM OF FOOD AT A MEAL! The system is called, apparently, "instinctive eating," and virtually every disease disappears when one does it.

This naturopath also said that only those people whose bodies are full of toxemia will have problems with parasitic worms if they eat raw meat, that the worms feed on the toxemia and not on the healthy cells. I do not guarantee that this is true; I am merely telling you what this naturopath told me; he sounded like a very intelligent man who had researched the subject carefully and extensively but I do not personally guarantee the accuracy of this assertion! I hope this naturopath writes a book himself to tell us all what he has discovered. He also told me that those races of people who live on raw meat, do not get colon cancer, though the medical theory is that since meat has not got the fibers to clean out the colon, people who eat mostly meat and other non-fibrous foods are prone to colon cancer. Apparently this theory only applies to cooked meat.

So come to your own conclusions about raw meat; it seems a natural enough sort of food, evidence apparently shows that it is quite healthful; I'm not going to be a fanatic vegetarian and condemn it. I am not personally in the habit of eating it, but neither am I going to condemn it.

Well after this pleasant digression, let's get back to John Tobe and his writings. Tobe was an avid gardener and farmer and operated a nursery for many years, and wrote extensively on these subjects also. As well, in the 1950s he became one of the few persons able to obtain permission from the government of Pakistan as well as an invitation from the Mir of Hunza, to visit Hunza, the small country in the great Karakorum mountain range whose inhabitants are reputed to enjoy the best health and longest lives of any people in the world. Tobe wrote about his trip there, in a book called *Hunza: Adventures in a Land of Paradise*. He did indeed note the healthy appearance of the Hunza people; he said that they walked with a grace and power that he had never seen before and were extremely remarkable for their endurance, intelligence and cheerful dispositions; they did indeed appear to be enjoying their lives far more than most of the more "civilized" people, though they had a hard and simple life, with little technology or luxuries; for food they had mostly only apricots, wheat chapaties and vegetables which they worked hard to grow on their scarce farmland. Tobe found them to be in nearly ideal health, the only common problem being with eyesight, due to spending so much time in their smoke-filled houses in winter; apparently they had not developed any good ventilation systems to take care of that problem. Also, he said, they had recently taken to eating refined salt, and some diseases were beginning to appear on this account. Tobe noted well the dilemma: people want health and intelligence and great happiness and long life, but they also want rich and abundant food, refined, cooked and processed food, and they want labor-saving devices and all sorts of modern technological conveniences; and the two appear to be incompatible.

Tobe had no college degrees and he explained why: that all a college degree will prove, would be that he had allowed that institution to indoctrinate him and control his thinking along their desired lines for so many years. How was that anything to be proud of? He preferred to read and study and educate himself on his own. He gained much valuable knowledge by such independent study and used it to help many people until his death in 1979 from cancer. He was a very good and intelligent man, a true benefactor of humanity, as proven by the fact that at one time the Canadian government prosecuted him for fraud in connection with a book he wrote on natural treatment of cataracts in the eyes. You may ask, why did he die of cancer if he was such a health expert? Well, certain Natural Hygienic writers say that, while he believed in and advocated a raw food diet, he did not practice it very consistently himself and frequently ate in delicatessens and such like places. He did not claim to be a perfect raw foodist in his books; he said he generally ate one cooked meal a day, the other two all raw. So that is the reason why, some say, he died of cancer.

Dick Gregory is another very well known and influential promoter of raw food diets and fasting. He has many outstanding accomplishments to his credit; star long-distance runner in high school and college, famous comedian and entertainer earning millions of dollars, a leader of the civil rights movement and author of several books; but in his book Dick Gregory's Natural Diet for Folks Who Eat: Cookin' with Mother Nature, he describes his experiences of rejuvenation and spiritual awakening through fasting and raw food diet as the greatest accomplishments of his life. He is now promoting a line of nutritional and health products called "Dick Gregory's Bahamian Diet."

T.C. Fry must be the most active and influential promoter of Natural Hygiene today; in addition to numerous books he also publishes a monthly magazine called "Healthful Living." He has also made up a correspondence course in natural hygiene which offers graduates a Ph.D. degree. The most memorable piece of his that I have read, was his book *The Myth of Medicine*, which explains how many drugs appear to have curative effects by suppressing the symptoms and driving the causes of the disease "underground" in the body, where eventually they spring up again to cause even worse diseases than those which the drugs were used to suppress. He has also recently published an eye-opening pamphlet on AIDS, which lists a number of immuno-deficiency diseases described in the medical literature long before we heard of AIDS; things like SCID (Severe Combined Immune Deficiency) and IDS (Immune Deficiency Syndrome). The medical literature gave the causes of these older immune-deficiency diseases as things like drugs, radiation and cytotoxins, which of course means "cell poisons"—which can include alcohol, food additives, tobacco smoke, pesticide residues—all these things poison the cells!

So, I wrote to a local AIDS information organization and asked them, 1. What's the difference between AIDS and IDS, SCID, CID and so forth, and 2. How does a doctor know for sure that someone has AIDS instead of IDS, SCID or CID, and, 3. How do the doctors know for sure that HIV virus causes AIDS, and that AIDS is not caused by the drugs, radiation and cytotoxins that caused the former, less-publicized immune-deficiency diseases? They wrote me back and said these were good questions, they couldn't really tell me the answer, and that actually there's no proof that HIV virus causes AIDS! T.C. Fry's opinion was that AIDS is a hoax created by the medical establishment to sell drugs, raise money for research on drugs and vaccines for AIDS and scare people into accepting population control measures and infringement on civil rights and liberties in the name of "preventing the spread of AIDS." He points out that more people die every year from sleeping pill overdoses, than from AIDS. And from what I have heard, it's apparently quite posssible to overcome

AIDS if a person will adopt a healthful lifestyle. Viktoras Kulvinskas reported good success in New York, helping AIDS victims overcome it with wheatgrass juice, live food diets and generally healthy lifestyle. A number of other healers report good success helping AIDS patients get better, through fasting, natural diet, appropriate herbs, exercise, etc. The key seems to be, to build up your health rather than take drugs to kill your bug. AIDS patients usually have miserably unhealthy lifestyles. T.C. Fry points out that 2/3 of reported AIDS deaths are among junkies who shoot drugs! That's enough to kill someone right there; who needs an "AIDS virus"?

Dr. Jack Goldstein is another outstanding natural hygienic author and lecturer. He suffered from medically-incurable colitis which made his life miserable for many years until he discovered natural hygiene. He tells his story in his book *Triumph over Disease through Fasting and Natural Diet.*

Johanna Brandt was author of the popular little book, *The Grape Cure.* She suffered from stomach cancer, and found that so long as she ate, it continued worsening until it threatened to kill her. She fasted over and over, finding that while fasting the cancer stopped growing and began to shrink; but when at last she had to resume eating or starve to death, the cancer would always begin growing once more as she ate. Finally she discovered that on a diet of exclusively grapes, the cancer stopped growing and began to shrink until finally it was unnoticeable. She then discovered that adding a few other raw foods to her diet did not stimulate the growth of the cancer again.

Dr. Kristine Nolfi was another cancer victim, breast cancer in this case, who found relief through a raw vegetarian diet. She found that so long as she ate exclusively raw foods, the cancer remained in remission, undetectable. But as soon as she ate any cooked foods, the cancer would flare up and begin growing again. Being a medical doctor, she put her experience to good use in helping thousands of other cancer sufferers to gain similar remissions of their conditions, for which she was viciously persecuted by medical colleagues. Her story is told in her book, *The Miracles of Living Foods*.

A similar story was told me by a woman from southern California. Her friend had cancer, so the two of them went to Ann Wigmore's Hippocrates Health Institute to learn how to eat wheat grass, bean sprouts and organic fruit. On this diet, her friend's cancer went into remission so she was no longer troubled by it. But after a while, her friend decided that, Jesus Christ, if I have to live on this damned bunny food the rest of my life, I'd rather be dead. So she started enjoying pizzas and hamburgers and such-like stuff again; her cancer flared up and grew rapidly and a few months later she was dead.

Morris Krok, from South Africa, is another outstanding raw foodist author, very much of a spiritual bent. His book *Kindred Soul* is a visionary and utopian work depicting a future human society of superior health, with advanced wisdom and great psychic and spiritual attainments, based around cultivation of fruit trees and fruitarian diet. He is also proficient in Hatha yoga and an accomplished marathon runner. I would name *Fruit, the Food and Medicine for Man* as his most inspiring, well-done book; I have met several spiritualistically-inclined raw fooders who say that this is the book that made them feel they just had to do it!

Dr. O.L.M. Abramowski was an Australian medical docto: who in middle age suffered from hardening of the arteries and a general loss of vigor and ability to work. But when he took up a raw vegetarian diet, he was restored to better health than he had ever known before, better than even as a young man. He tells his story in his booklet, *Fruitarian Diet and Physical Rejuvenation*. A memorable chapter of this booklet told of an experiment he conducted at his hospital. He divided his patients, suffering from various and sundry diseases, at random into two groups. The first group, he kept on standard hospital cooked food diet and drug therapy. The second group were taken off all drugs and given only fresh raw fruit to eat. Then, like your typical scientist, satisfying his curiosity by playing like toys with other peoples' lives, he sat back to see what would happen. Several weeks later, the experiment was forced into an untimely and inconclusive end when the head nurse rebelliously refused to administer any drugs and cooked foods to the patients in the first group any longer, because, she said, it was clearly killing them. Therefore, to this day there is still no accurate data available on the average length of time required to kill a patient via drugs and standard hospital diet; but by writing his booklet Dr. Abramowski nevertheless contributed something to human knowledge.

John A. Crawford, N.D., "Johnny Papaya," of Hawaii, is another raw fooder with whom I had some correspondence some years ago. He advocated the RAF diet, signifying not the Royal Air Force, but Raw Alkaline Fruit. He said that all vegetables and seeds contain poisons and should not be eaten. In addition, tomatoes, being of the Nightshade family, contain poisons and should not be eaten. In addition, he said that all citrus and acidic fruits are too harsh, too sour and acidic, and should not be eaten. I believe he lived on just papayas and melons and very little if anything else. He called himself a Teacher of Morality and Natural Living, and strongly asserted that sex should only be indulged in for the purpose of reproducing children. His teachings will certainly never be popular, though they may be wise.

Kevin Edds is the author of How to Live 100s of Years which describes his remarkable improvement of health as a result of following Prof. Arnold Ehret's teachings. He is a Mormon and in his book devotes a good deal of effort to demonstrating the compatibility of Mormonism and raw foodism, being in this respect similar to raw fooders of other religions and spiritual philosophies who often devote considerable effort to proving the compatibility of raw foodism with their religion or philosophy, usually with the hope of converting all the other members of their religion to raw foodism. I did this myself; when I became a raw foodist I was a member of a society called the Divine Light

Mission, and the first thing I wanted to do was to convert all the other members of Divine Light Mission to raw foodism. I thought at first that they would go for it, because they had been open-minded and truth-seekers enough to respond rationally to our Guru's offer to show us God. "I can show you God," he had said. "Take my Knowledge and meditate on it and if it makes you happy, continue; if not, leave it." It was an offer that no rational person could refuse, and I found that meditating on his Knowledge made one happier and more rational still. So I thought all the other members of the Divine Light Mission would see what a good idea raw food diet was and would right away take it up when I told them about my experience with it. To my surprised disappointment, I found them all to be totally prejudiced against it, coming up with the most absolutely ridiculous and feeble-minded rationalizations why they shouldn't do it. And it is the same with the members of any other religion, society, group, cult, organization, etc. So I suggest raw fooders not bother to try too hard to convert all the other members of their religion or group or cult, because though they may have an interest or two in common with you, you will inevitably find that they are no more rational or truth-seekers in an over-all sort of way, than any group of the public at large of similar size taken at random. There is a certain very small percentage of rational and sincerely truth-seeking people scattered throughout the population and no group or religion or cult contains a higher percentage of them than any other random population sample. So the best thing is to broadcast your truth to the public at large, don't get your hopes up too high for the other members of your religion or cult, and a certain small percentage will respond positively and often they will be the people you least expected to; whereas the people you most hope and expect will understand, will usually disappoint you bitterly.

The title of Mr. Edds's book refers to his belief in the theory, common to religiously-inclined raw foodists, that Methuselah and other Biblical figures with reported life-spans in the 900-year range, enjoyed such fabulous longevity because of their raw food diet of "fruits and herbs," upon which people allegedly lived, before the Flood, according to the express orders of God. As previously noted, raw fooders of this persuasion get a lot of mileage out of the fact that the Bible doesn't mention cooking and meat-eating until after the Flood. So far, though, no modern raw foodist has lived significantly past 100; most have lived close to the average length of life, 70 or 80 or so.

Paul Bragg was a well-known health promoter who became introduced to natural healing at a sanitorium in Switzerland where he had gone trying to recover from tuberculosis. Through fasting, sunbathing and natural diet there he did indeed make a complete recovery, and he then devoted the rest of his long life to studying and teaching health improvement, calling himself a "life extension specialist." His writings are very strong and inspiring, advocating exercise, deep breathing, fasting, sunbathing, and a diet of 80% uncooked fruits, vegetables, nuts and seeds. He remained very vigorous and active until his death at age 95, reportedly in a surfing accident.

Hannah Hurnard wrote a book called *Fruitarianism, Compassionate Way to Transformed Health,* advocating a diet of nothing but fruits as the only way to live perfectly in accord with the ideal of not killing anything, because even when we eat the leaves, stems, roots and seeds of plants we are still killing something that was created for other purposes than to die between the grinding teeth of greedy human beings; but the fruits of plants are created for the express purpose of being plucked and eaten by humans and other animal-like creatures, so that the seed would be carried some distance from the parent plant to reproduce its kind. In this fruitarian diet, Ms. Hurnard included not only apples, peaches, oranges and other sweet juicy things that we commonly think of as fruits, but also various vegetables which by strict botanical definition must likewise be classified as fruits, such things as pumpkins, squashes, cucumbers, peppers and so forth. I have recently been informed that, for reasons as yet unknown to me, Ms. Hurnard has abandoned fruitarianism in favor of macrobiotics.

Professor Edmond Bordeaux Szekely is well known as a revivalist of ancient Essene teachings, which reportedly taught an uncooked vegetarian diet as most conducive to health plus mental and spiritual development. The famous "Essene bread" consists of whole grains soaked in water and sprouted, then ground to flour, pounded into flat cakes and placed in the hot sun for slow low-temperature baking. It must have been this sort of bread which inspired the expression, "bread is the staff of life," because I understand that the modern white bread, enriched to build strong bodies twelve ways, has been found to kill rats in short order when they are given nothing but water and this sort of bread to live on.

Stanley Burroughs is author of a very fine book called *Healing for the Age of Enlightenment*, which promotes raw food diet, color therapy, and the "Master Cleanser," which is a lemonade made up of water, lemon juice, maple syrup and cayenne pepper which some people like to drink while otherwise fasting because it keeps one's energy up while still allowing the body to do a thorough cleansing job. Color therapy is a system of radiating the body with lights of various colors; each color is supposed to have a certain specific therapeutic effect. One friend of mine, who is highly psychic, has tried it and says it is quite powerful; that the colored lights affect the etheric body which in turn affects the physical body.

Burroughs must be a true and dedicated friend of all humanity because last I heard, at around age 70, he had to spend several years in jail in California (for "healing without a license"), which state apparently has an extremely vicious and reactionary medical establishment, probably because so much of the modern natural healing movement got started there. In a book called *Naked Empress, or the Great Medical Hoax*, Hans Reusch tells the story of how the modern character of the medical establishment originated, grew and developed. Reusch in turn quoted the story from a hard-to-get book called *The Drug Story* by Morris Bealle. Apparently, back in the 19th century, "Old Bill" Rockefeller discovered that there were fabulous profits to be made by bottling up crude petroleum and peddling it as a "cure for cancer." His son, John D. Rockefeller, continued this line of business, calling his little bottle of crude oil "Nujol" and selling it as a "cure for constipation." Apparently 1/5¢ worth of crude oil could be sold wholesale to druggists for 23¢, making it a business with a 10,000% profit. Quick to recognize a lucrative opportunity, John D. Rockefeller Sr. and Jr. invested heavily in drug-manufacturing enterprises and set up charitable foundations to fund medical education and medical research which would promote drug therapy, and through influence in government and the mass media, set out to stamp out homeopathy, naturopathy, herbology, midwifery and in general all forms of health care except "the religion of modern medicine," to borrow Dr. Robert Mendehlson's phrase, which religion of course is totally dependent upon very expensive drugs. So it is enlightening to know that the totally unscientific and irrational rejection of all natural and drugless health care systems by the universities, mass media and government agencies isn't just some sort of strange accident but has been carefully and systematically cultivated with big, big, big money. If you've got enough money to push your message into people's minds from all sides day and night, all their lives, and can publish your message in the slickest of magazines and the most authoritative-looking, expensive volumes under the color of highest scholarly authority, you can almost fool God himself. Incidentally, Mr. Bealle reported that John D. Rockefeller Sr. and Jr. weren't fool enough to take their own drugs; they retained homeopathic physicians for their personal health care.

Marcia Acciardo is author of a popular new-agey raw-food recipe book, published by Viktoras Kulvinskas and called *Light Eating for Survival*. Its page after page of delicious recipes prove that raw foodists can, if they want, spend just as much time in the kitchen whomping up complicated, intricate and tasty dishes as any French chef. Some people say they'd like to try raw foodism but don't know any raw food recipes; if you're one of those, this is the book for you!

Sheila Andrews is author of another raw food recipe book called *The No-cook Fruitarian Recipe Book.*

Marti Wheeler, a Natural Hygienist, is also author of a raw food recipe book, published by T.C. Fry's Life Science publishing company.

Joshua Rainbow, from Kauai, Hawaii, is a notable fruitarian author and one of the most original-minded. He writes at one point that, as a teen-ager, his father told him he had to work, that "you can't just eat and make love;" so he set out to discover how to live so that all he had to do was eat and make love. He has made the striking and original observation that life and death are said to be the two extremes, but actually life is always right in the middle and death lies at both the extremes; for instance you can kill yourself by starving or over-eating, by being too hot or too cold, and so forth.

There have been some stories of people whose teeth began falling out when they tried to live on only citrus fruits or only juicy fruits. This would be enough to make me quit such fruitarianism in a damn quick hurry if it happened, which it hasn't; but Joshua Rainbow claims that is a good sign: your spirit is becoming more peaceful and abandoning its murderous dental weapons! I'm not convinced of that, but I very much enjoyed reading the books of such an original thinker as Joshua Rainbow.

Bianca Leonardo is president of the American Vegetarian Society and co-author with Scott J. Gregory of *Conquering AIDS Now!,* a book on natural treatmeant of Acquired Immune Deficiency Syndrome, AIDS, the great Black Plague of the 1980s. Apparently quite a few AIDS victims have recovered as a result of following treatments such as are described in Leonardo and Gregory's book. Now when somebody recovers from a disease under drugless treatment methods, fasting, improved diet, etc., the medical doctors call it "spontaneous remission;" for unknown and mysterious reasons the diseased condition has gotten better. The reasons are unknown and mysterious because they won't acknowledge that anything but drugs, radiation and surgery can possibly have any effect on the progress of a disease. Once in a while you hear, in the mass-media news reports, that an AIDS victim has had a "spontaneous remission" and it's well worth speculating that some of these "spontaneous remissions" were due to treatments such as described in Conquering AIDS Now!

Leonardo advocates that ripe fruits and vegetables be called "suncooked" rather than "uncooked," as the former denotes a state of completeness and perfection whereas the latter, or the word "raw" denotes an unfulfilled sort of condition—incomplete. For the same reason, some raw-foodists prefer to refer to "live foods" rather than "raw food"—it emphasizes something positive rather than something negative. An eater of "raw food" sounds like a filthy barbarian, while an eater of "suncooked foods" sounds like a noble and enlightened soul, besides probably being artistic and poetic also!

Personally I have gone on talking about "raw foods" because I have been afraid that if I talked about "live foods" or "suncooked foods" or "foods baked to perfection in the life-giving solar fire" I would sound like a member of some quasi-messianic cult that talked in a weird jargon all its own; my greatest desire all my life has been to be just a perfectly ordinary person and I have just wanted to use the simplest, commonest term available that would get the point across. And living on a raw food diet does indeed help you to feel like just a perfectly normal, ordinary person, no different from the trees or birds or fishes or cats or dogs or any other of the myriad common living things that populate the planet. Trouble is, when you become a normal, ordinary person, you find out that damn near the whole human race has become very, very abnormal!

David A. Phillips, Ph.D., from Australia, wrote a natural-hygienically oriented book called From Soil to Psyche telling why the biologically natural human diet of uncooked vegetarian foods can enable humankind to unfold its full potential of health and culture.

Teresa Mitchell is author of an extremely inspiring story published by the Ehret Literature Publishing Company in a booklet called *Roads to Health and Happiness,* describing her experiences in following Arnold Ehret's teachings.

Fred Hirsch was proprietor of the Ehret Literature Publishing Company for many years and accomplished the tremendous great work of selling over a quarter of a million copies of Prof. Ehret's books worldwide, and was a fine writer on health and fasting himself.

Don Weaver is a Natural Hygienist and co-author with John Hamaker of one of the most remarkable and important books of the 20th century, called *The Survival of Civilization.* The thesis of this book is that now, this minute, as I write this, we are in a period of rapid climate change leading to another Ice Age. This period of change began about 1975 and will culminate in the resumption of a full Ice-Age climate by about 1995. The major reasons for this climate change are two-fold: involving the progressive demineralization of most soils around the world since the end of the last Ice Age, and the rapid increase of carbon dioxide, CO_2, in the air as a result both of the demineralization of soils and the burning of immense quantities of fossil fuels. As CO_2 increases in the air, a Greenhouse Effect takes place: more of the sun's heat is retained by the atmosphere than formerly, thus making the air warmer in those areas where the Greenhouse Effect is able to occur.

The Greenhouse Effect is mostly a phenomenon of the tropics, and of the lower temperate zones in summer (lower referring to their degree of latitude; the equator is at 0° latitude making it the "lowest" location on Earth; the two poles are both at 90° latitude, making them the "highest" spots, for the purpose of the present discussion!), because that is where most of sunlight is! At the higher latitudes the sunlight is very much weaker and so there isn't much Greenhouse Effect there, contrary to the short-sighted, official and conventional scientific viewpoint that the Greenhouse Effect is causing the whole world to warm up uniformly, or even causing the poles to warm up more than the tropics.

As a result of the Greenhouse Effect, the tropics heat up, and as they heat up, more water evaporates out of the tropical oceans which as you know so very well, cover most of the tropics! But the poles don't heat up nearly so much—so a more exaggerated pressure/temperature differential than formerly is set up between tropical and polar air masses. This results in more violent interaction between these air masses, producing windier and stormier weather in general, and speeding up the general circulation of air masses from the tropics to the poles and back. Now when the waterlogged tropical air gets up into the higher latitudes, the water condenses out to form clouds and as a result of a denser-than-before cloud cover, the higher latitudes thus actually tend to cool down because of this Greenhouse Effect! And as more snow than before tends to fall out of these clouds, this starts the ice caps to growing, and as the ice caps grow, more sunlight on the average than before is reflected back into empty space by their dazzling white surfaces, rather than absorbed by the darker colors of soil, vegetation etc. And so this further helps to cool down the high latitudes and help the ice caps at the poles to grow still further!

So now you see how an Ice Age starts as a result of the Greenhouse Effect and the only remaining major question is, how did Ice Ages in the past get started, assuming there was no technologically-advanced society of human beings on the planet at that time to dig up huge amounts of coal and oil to run their motor cars, electricity-generating facilities and other techno-gadgetry? The answer lies in the progressive demineralization of soils during interglacial intervals of nice weather. The glaciers of the Ice Age, as they slowly creep over the landscape with mighty and irresistible force, crush and grind uncountable billions of tons of all species of rock to dust and gravel beneath their relentless bulk. Rivers of melt water flowing out from beneath the glaciers carry this fine-particled rock dust far and wide over the land, and the great howling winds of the harsh and rugged Ice Age climate further serve to distribute this rock dust to every nook and cranny of the globe. Thus the soils of the world receive from this action, a vast and abundant bounty of the vital minerals of life, upon which the soil microbes and other miniscule forms of soil life can thrive in their countless teeming trillions! This creates a rich and fertile soil upon which the higher plants and forest trees can take firm root and grow to their fullest magnificent potential! Now to build their carbon-based organic bodies, the trees and plants and soil microbes absorb zillions of tons of CO^2 yearly from out the atmosphere, thus reducing the Greenhouse Effect, moderating the climate and precipitating all the world into an interlude of comparatively pleasant and warm weather known as the Interglacial Age! These Interglacial Ages last about ten thousand years, until, via gradual leaching and erosion, the soil mineral supply deposited in the last Ice Age is finally exhausted. Then the population of soil microbes drops; the forests die and burn away, the CO^2 count of the air zooms upward like a nuclear-powered rollercoaster and another Ice Age begins.

And where are we now in the process? Hamaker and Weaver figure that we are in a brief transition period, about 20 years long, between the end of the last Interglacial and the beginning of the next Ice Age. We see the signs of the change all around us now—forests sickening and dying, huge forest fires, records for extreme weather of all sorts falling right and left—we're having heat, cold, floods, droughts, snow, and wind like never before. The Great Lakes and the Great Salt Lake are rising; surely something is at hand. A massive Greenhouse Effect will warm up the whole world and make it hot enough for Fire Ants to live EVERYWHERE. (There's these two creatures immune to radiation, you know, the Cockroaches and the Fire Ants, and at first they will all enjoy feasting on the rotting bodies of all the dead people; plenty of corpses to go around. But then when they've gobbled up all the dead people and dogs and cats and cows and so forth, well, they will turn to fighting each other! So it will come down to a great all-out war between the Cockroaches and the Fire Ants for who is going to RULE THE WORLD. Who will win? All the smart money is on the Fire Ants. Anyone who's ever been to Texas knows that, beyond the slightest shadow of a doubt, the Fire Ants are the baddest, meanest, most vicious creature to ever walk the face of this Earth. Obviously they are destined to Rule the World!)

Now I've embellished what Hamaker and Weaver say a little

bit, here and there, but that's the general idea. Hamaker and Weaver proposed a way by which we can maintain the Interglacial climate and prevent the unpleasant events described above. That is, we can do what the glaciers do!—grind up zillions of tons of rocks and gravel and broadcast the dust over our gardens, farms, forests—in a word, everywhere. This would restore the populations of soil microbes and trees which would absorb the excess CO_2 in the air and thus we would maintain the Interglacial climate upon which civilization-as-we-know-it depends absolutely. Some people have taken up the call to do this—the best way to quickly find out more is to read a magazine called *Soil Remineralization*— the address will be found in the back of this book!

Buckminster Fuller read John Hamaker and Don Weaver's book, *The Survival of Civilization*, shortly before his death, and called it "well done—completely convincing." I think it is too. I'll put the address where you can get it at the back of this book too.

Ray Swangkee writes under the name of "The Peacock," "The Goat," "The Great White Workhorse" and various other creatures, and he ran for U.S.A President in 1984 under the slogan, "Vote for the Goat!" He is a raw fooder with sweeping plans to reorganize human life so we can all be healthier, happier, and get out of debt. His many books cover all aspects of his plans in great detail.

Another concern of Ray's has been to rationalize the spelling of the written English language. Hee haz duvelupd u nq sistum uv speling funetiklee wich hee kawlz "Nq Ingglish." Hee haz u bouk kawld *Rqlz Foor Fasting* publishd in Nq Ingglish that hee wil send free tq eneewun hq riitz tq him reekwesting it. Hee awlsoo haz menee uthrr bouks foor saal. Hiz adres iz: The Peacock, Angel Ridge, King's Mountain, Kentucky 40442.

Dr. Norman Walker was another very notable raw-foodist author; I hear that he died recently at the age of 109. He is especially notable for his advocacy of drinking large amounts of vegetable juices, both for treating diseases and maintaining excellent health. He was the inventor of the Norwalk juicer, the very best juicer ever made; costs around a thousand bucks new and lasts a lifetime.

Gabriel Cousens, M.D., is author of the new-age blockbuster, *Spiritual Nutrition and the Rainbow Diet*, which all sorts of the more new-agey, raw foodists are praising to the skies as the great new classic and definitive work on diet. In this book, Dr. Cousens introduces the concept of the SOEF, the Subtle Organizing Energy Field which sets the pattern for the physical body and thus controls the health of the physical body. Live foods help to build a stronger, better organized SOEF which in turn is able to maintain a healthier body with clearer, more organized and harmonious mental functions. This is the point I want to stress most of all, over and over: the raw food diet transforms you in a way which you could not previously imagine. As a conventional cooked food eater, when you hear the words "better health," you imagine yourself as you are now but free of obvious disease symptoms. But besides usually cleaning up all disease symptoms, the raw food diet also makes you feel lighter, clearer, more truly alive and dynamic in a way that the lifelong cooked eater absolutely cannot imagine. Raw food eaters really do live in a different, more real world. Their attitudes and opinions become transformed, energized by the reality of the Life-Force, whereas in most cooked food eaters, their attitudes and desires and opinions are programmed into their minds by parents, school, friends, clubs and organizations, etc. and thus come from a very limited and superficial reality indeed and not from the deeper wisdom and reality of Nature at all. I won't say that a raw food diet totally cleanses and deconditions your consciousness, as many raw fooders retain strong attachments to religious dogmas and doctrines, and it doesn't end the problem of emotional energy blockages which some people suffer from, but the one great thing that it *always* seems to do, is to reconnect a person to Nature and make them aware that health, strength, wisdom and happiness come from harmony with Nature and not from technological advancement or education.

Dr. Cousens introduces the concept of the Rainbow Diet,

which involves eating daily, foods of all the colors of the rainbow, for fully balanced nutritional energies which of course would tend to create a balanced SOEF or energy field. As well, he discusses the ancient Indian Ayurvedic medical system, which classifies people into three major types, or doshas, and suggests which foods will be found to be best for each type. Dr. Cousens has obviously studied this matter of diet very extensively, has studied fasting also, has good perception of how these matters tie in with the evolution and development of the mind and soul, and in this book presents his knowledge.

Harvey and Marilyn Diamond are authors of *Fit for Life*, an excellent popular presentation of Natural Hygiene. I hear it is now the all-time bestselling popular health and diet book. It has excellent information on the body's natural cycles of cleansing, appropriation and assimilation and how to cooperate with them for good health, and valuable information on food combining, and page after page of recipes for healthful meals. A great book to give all your friends and relatives for Christmas presents!

And finally, *Essie Honiball* is author of *I Live on Fruit*, which tells of her recovery from a terribly weakened condition via the fruit diet, and tells of numerous other South African raw foodists and fruitarians as well. One interesting story in her book, is of a child raised as a fruitarian, who enjoyed a natural proficiency in telepathy; for instance, he was readily able to understand the conversation of a Bantu woman though he didn't know a word of Bantu. Essie tells how she converted her husband to fruitarianism, though he had no interest in changing his conventional diet. She began serving him fruit with all meals, then gradually reducing the amount of cooked foods, then occasionally serving an all-fruit meal, then making most meals all-fruit. Finally one morning she served him a breakfast of conventional ham-and-eggs type food, and his immediate reaction was, "Do I have to eat this slop? Can't I just have fruit?" And she did it all with no preaching!

OKAY—So there are a couple dozen or so 20th century raw

food advocates who have distinguished themselves in some way by writing and publishing about it, and the summaries of their writings should give you some grasp of the range of ideas and points of view within the over-all raw foodist community.

Of course there are many other fine raw foodists who have done and are doing great work, and I haven't included them all because I don't know them all and my purpose here has been only to review the major writers whose writings have shaped the character of the present raw foodist community and also had much influence on the entire natural health care movement. If you want to know more about the many other fine raw foodists, then I suggest read Viktoras Kulvinskas and Richard Tasca Jr.'s book, *Life in the 21st Century*, because they've got most of them in there.

Now a word about constipation, which many people seem to suffer from considering the booming sales of over-the-counter laxatives, and which is said to be the precursor to most other diseases, since it allows accumulation of abnormal amounts of wastes within the body. There are many ideas what to do about it; the best thing I have ever found is running. Run a mile or two a day and I don't think you will ever have the problem. Since running is such a normal part of natural living, I think we could even say that constipation often develops due to lack of running. I remember when I was running daily in high school, in training for track, I never had a cold or flu though I was eating all sorts of junk food; this was the only time in my life before becoming a raw foodist, that I was consistently healthy. The running also made me want to eat less, so as to feel comfortable while running, and I'm sure that helped me to be healthier at that time too.

Running is another one of those things that makes you realize how little you really need to be happy. When you're in shape for it, nothing makes you happier, makes you feel better, than running five miles. I had a friend in California who said, "I don't feel spiritual unless I run every day." Warning: run on grass or dirt roads, not on pavement. If you run on pavement, you're almost certain to get knee trouble sooner or later, even with expensive modern running shoes.

ICE COLD, HARD, RATIONAL & OBJECTIVE SCIENTIFIC EVIDENCE OF THE HARMS OF COOKING

4

RAW FOODISM HAS SPREAD mostly because it makes sense. It makes horse sense and common sense and some of the witty types say it makes dollars and cents, because fruit and vegetables are cheaper than meat and it also saves you thousands of dollars on doctor bills, dentist bills, and drugs of both the recreational and prescription variety. Prescription drugs of course you don't buy anymore as a raw foodist because you don't get sick; recreational drugs lose much of their attraction because raw food diet is a better high than even LSD, to say nothing of marijuana. You also save money on gas or electricty to run your stove, and you tend to prefer to walk or ride a bicycle so you save money on gasoline also. The world of Nature becomes far more interesting than artificial entertainments so you tend to spend less on movies too. On the other hand, you are likely to develop a strong desire to convert the world, and end up spending all that money you saved on publishing books and pamphlets to spread your propaganda!

Every person whose thought processes have not become hopelessly corrupted by cooked-food addiction and spurious health theories, always recognizes immediately as soon as they hear about raw foodism, that of course it is the most natural and therefore bound to be the healthiest and why didn't I think of it myself a long time ago? However, true science and intuitive understanding never contradict, and there is in fact a good deal of hard scientific data to show the superior health benefits of a raw food diet, and some of the more intelligent, educated and respectable raw foodists are constantly gathering more such data, so that for a person capable of unprejudiced thought, the evidence for the superiority of the raw food diet is now absolutely irrefutable.

So now let's look at some of this hard, cold, objective and scientific data.

For example, in Dr. Ann Wigmore's book *Be Your Own Doctor*, she says:

> "Cancer growths and sores appear in practically every part of the body and take a long time to heal. Since the body creates these conditions, it is essential to eliminate the food which feeds their development. From his long experience, Dr. Earp-Thomas was fully convinced that when cooked food was eaten it permitted tumors and growths to build within the body. Yet when living food was substituted, these tumors and growths immediately began to shrink for lack of nourishment. The most thrilling experience I can recall was to see cancer cells taken from a human body and thriving on cooked food but unable to survive on that same food when it was uncooked."

Of course this pattern applies to the macrocosm as well as the microcosm! The cancerous growth on the planet—that modern human technocratic civilization has become—lives on cooked food! If people would return to natural eating, this cancer on the Earth could not survive.

Further on, in the same book, Dr. Wigmore reports:

"The experience of my good friend, John A. MacDonald, shows the power, the almost unbreakable strength for evil, in improper foods. Some years ago, John owned a pet shop which specialized in the raising of white mice. He sold mice by the thousands all over the world. In his enclosure for the mice, he had placed a large bale of hay. From the dried grass, the mice built a cooperative apartment house. They cut numerous tunnels through it, built hanging gardens, cliff-dwelling pueblos and wonderful balconies on which they raised their young in harmony. It was a happy existence of peace and plenty.

"John became concerned about the rising price of grain to feed his mice and was on the lookout for ways to cut costs. A neighbor who ran a rather sizeable boarding house offered to supply him daily with leftover scraps from her tables. John gladly accepted the opportunity to increase his profits. But when the leftover food was substituted for the grain, a blight seemed to settle over the mouse community. Eating the same food that human beings ate changed the complexion of the co-operative establishment. Quarrels broke out and battles raged through the baled-hay corridors. By the end of the week, dead mice littered the floor of the compound. Cannibalistic parents ate their young. The weaker mice were slain without provocation.

"Realizing that only disaster loomed ahead, John threw out the scraps of food and went back to grain. The result was quickly evident. No more mice were found dead or half-eaten. This is not an imaginary story. It is a documented history of facts. And what the food human beings ate did to the mice, it is evidently doing today in many disastrous ways to our children and adults in many of our communities."

Dr. Wigmore continued:

"Here is another incident to demonstrate the havoc of unsuitable food. It is the saga of two sister white cats having litters of kittens in the same bureau drawer one early May. They were both fed a mild, dry cat food mixed with freshly cut wheatgrass. Harmony reigned in that drawer as the eight kittens used any convenient spout that was available for the precious milk. The kittens did not know which of the cats was their mother.

"Then on May 25, responding to an advertisement on television, the mother cats were switched from their accustomed food to canned meat with no wheatgrass. The harmonious situation began to disrupt almost immediately. On May 31 the two mother cats were rolling on the floor clawing each other, bringing blood to their white fur. The canned meat was not served that evening, and in its place was the mild cat food with the wheatgrass. This feeding was continued and within a week the two mother cats once again sprawled out peacefully to co-operatively feed the youngsters. The experiment was repeated again to make sure this was the reason for the change in disposition of the mother cats. The results were the same."

In the same book, Dr. Wigmore makes the statement that cooking destroys up to 83% of the value of food. So, eating cooked food is like taking a job at $300 a week and, after taxes, getting $51 to take home to support your luxurious lifestyle.

In John Tobe's book *The Golden Treasury of Natural Health Knowledge*, there is a copy of a paper by Paul Kouchakoff, M.D., for the First International Congress of Microbiology, in Paris, in 1930. Dr. Kouchakoff's discovery concerned the leukocytes, the white blood cells. Apparently it was well known that immediately after a person ate, there was a sudden increase of white corpuscles in the blood. It was considered that this was a normal, physiological phenomenon. Dr. Kouchakoff discovered that this increase of the white corpuscles only occurred when cooked, artificially altered food was eaten; when natural raw food was eaten, no such increase of the white corpuscles occurred. Here are some of the key points of Dr. Kouchakoff's conclusions:

"After 300 experiments on ten individuals of different ages and sex, we have come to the following conclusions:
1. The augmentation of the number of white corpuscles and the alteration of the correlation of the percentage between them which takes place after every consumption of food, and was considered until now as a physiological phenomenon, is, in reality, a pathological one. It is called forth by the introduction into the

system of foodstuffs altered by means of a high temperature and by complicated treatments of ordinary products produced by nature.

2. After the consumption of foodstuffs produced by nature but altered by means of high temperature, an augmentation of the general number of white corpuscles, as well as a change in the correlation of this percentage, takes places.

3. It has been proved possible to take, without changing the blood formula, every kind of foodstuff which is habitually eaten now, but only by following this rule, viz.—that it must be taken along with raw products, according to a definite formula. (Author's note—as I recall, this formula was that the raw foods must be eaten first and must constitute at least 50% of the total meal.)

4. Blood examination can only have significance as a diagnosis if it is made on an empty stomach."

In his book *Pasteur Plagiarist Imposter!*, R.B. Pearson describes experiments done with cats by Dr. F.M. Pottenger and D.G. Simonsen. Incidentally, in addition to the aforementioned Pearson book, I have seen another book called *Bechamp or Pasteur?* which likewise asserts that Louis Pasteur was not the great discoverer that history makes him out to be—that all of Pasteur's alleged great discoveries were actually made by his contemporary, Bechamp, who was a far more able scientist; however Pasteur was far more adept at gaining favorable publicity and social popularity. For instance, one memorable section of this book dealt with Bechamp's discovery of microzymas—the smallest form of living matter. Apparently Bechamp discovered that when the body chemistry was in proper balance, the microzymas developed into the so-called "benign" bacteria, whereas in the improperly balanced body, they developed into the so-called "disease germs." Pasteur, apparently, in misappropriating this discovery, made the mistake of asserting that the "disease germs" were the cause of the disease, rather than the underlying imbalanced condition which allowed the microzymas to develop into disease germs. I believe that Dr. Wilhelm Reich made similar discoveries, except that he called "bions" what Bechamp called "microzymas."

To continue with Pottenger's cats, Pearson writes:

"They put two groups of cats on diets of meat and vegetables, identical in value, except that in one group the meat was given raw, and this group seemed to maintain normal good health throughout the experiments. In the other group the meat was all cooked, and this group showed an astonishing breakdown of health in ALL of the animals.

"They found every sign of lack of minerals, such as incomplete development of the skull or other bones, bowed legs, rickets, curvature of the spine, paralysis of the legs, convulsive seizure, thyroid abscesses, cyanosis of liver and kidneys, enlarged colon, and degeneration of the motor nerve ganglion cells throughout the spinal cord and brain stem, with some cells affected in the cerebellum and cerebral cortex.

"Strange to say none of the cats on raw meat had any of these troubles at all, yet millions of humans are afflicted with one or more of them, and have no conception of the cause, and neither have their doctors in most of the cases. They add, of these cats:

"The deficiency renders the experimental animals so deplete in important vitalizing factors that the third generation is unable to live beyond the period corresponding to childhood in the human being."

This experiment of Drs. Pottenger and Price is one of the most interesting pieces of objective evidence for the value of the raw food diet. The full text appears in the Appendix.

Lady Eve Balfour described some of the further ramifications of the Pottenger experiments in a report titled *The Cycle of Health*, originally published in the March 1979 "Quarterly Review" of the British Soil Association and a couple of years later in the "Toronto Inner Life" magazine:

"If nutrition is a cycle—a flow of vitalized materials from the soil and back to the soil again—then it must be studied as a whole, and any specialized study of the part must be recognized as a study of the part. Its relation to all other parts must never be lost sight of.

Given that our major contention is correct, we may in fact be led seriously astray if we attempt to diagnose cause and effect, in any manifestation of living organisms, without taking into consideration their relationship to this wider whole. It is therefore of great practical importance to discover if this cycle is purely hypothetical or if it exists in fact.

"I have recently come across strong supporting evidence for its existence in a summarized report, by Dr. F.M. Pottenger, of a feeding experiment on cats, printed in the *American Journal of Orthodontics and Oral Surgery*. The experiment extended over ten years and involved 900 animals.

"The main purpose was a comparison between cooked and raw food, though there were various subdivisions using different combinations, such as groups of cats fed on raw meat with pasteurized milk, and others on cooked meat with raw milk. The animals who received an all raw food diet, both milk and meat, remained healthy and bred normal litters from generation to generation, while all those for which cooked food formed the major portion of the diet, whether this were meat or milk, became progressively degenerate through succeeding generations. For example, 25% of abortions occurred in the first generation and 70% in the second. The animals also fell prey to the varied range of diseases, all listed in the report, and in many cases by the third generation, the kittens had become so degenerate that they failed to survive for six months. A further experiment with different kinds of milk produced the same results. The cats fed raw milk remained healthy and bred normally from generation to generation, while all those fed on other forms of milk suffered from increasing degrees of sickness, degeneration, and skeletal malformation in this order: pasteurized milk, evaporated milk, and sweetened condensed milk. In later experiments cats whose general metabolism had been deranged by the cooked food were returned to a raw food diet. Complete regeneration, where it was not too late to achieve this, took four generations. This is a striking parallel to the experience of organic cultivators with plants.

"Now here is the part of these experiments which particularly concerns farmers and gardeners. After we performed these experiments the pens in which all these animals were housed lay fallow for several months. Weeds sprang up in each pen. The fact that the weeds grew so luxuriantly in the pen which housed the raw meat and raw milk fed animals, as compared with those which grew in the other pens, led us to perform another experiment.

"This experiment consisted of planting two kinds of beans in each pen, and the report contains a photograph showing these beans growing in four pens previously occupied by cats fed on the four milk diets mentioned above, namely raw milk, pasteurized milk, evaporated milk, and sweetened condensed milk. The growth of the crops followed exactly the same pattern as the health of the cats, and was in the same order—vigorously healthy beans in the raw milk pen, less good in the pasteurized, very poor in the evaporated and practically no growth at all in the sweetened condensed milk pen.

"The report ends with this extremely significant statement: 'The principles of growth and development are easily altered by heat and oxidation, which kill living cells at every stage of the life process from the soil, through the plant and through the animal. Change is not only shown in the immediate generation but as a *germ plasm injury which manifests itself in subsequent generations of plants and animals.'*

"The important thing about these experiments is not that heat kills living cells, but that devitalized food, when fed to an animal, could start a train of malnutrition that continues to manifest its effects right around the cycle. For when food was devitalized, not only did the cats which fed on it become devitalized, but the soil to which their excreta was returned was able to produce only devitalized plants. Vital living food, on the other hand, produced vital healthy cats whose excreta in its turn produced vital soil capable of producing vigorous healthy plants. From these facts it seems to me that we must draw the conclusion that plants can only reach their maximum vitality when grown in fully vitalized soil, and that soil can only reach its maximum vitality when it is fed with the waste products of fully vitalized plants and animals.

"Is it surprising then, that we set up a vicious circle when we first feed our soil on the lifeless products of the factory, then subject the weakened plants that result to every kind of life-destroying poison powder and spray, then feed them to our livestock—often further devitalized by heat processing—and finally partake ourselves of food derived from such plants and animals, usually further devitalized by various methods of sterilization or processing?

"It is against this destructive vicious circle that the ever growing number of organic cultivators are in revolt. They endeavor to substitute for it an ever-mounting spiral of increased fertility by seeking to operate the nutrition cycle in the opposite and creative direction, fostering the living principle in all its phases. This is why they lay such stress on growing their own seed, or buying it only from other organic cultivators. It is why, too, they endeavor as far as possible to feed their livestock and themselves on their own produce, for they know that soil, seed and animals, and their waste products all go together; and that maximum health and vitality, with the disease resistance that goes with it, cannot be built up in one generation, or from good seed alone.

"Many examples exist to confirm the truth of this. Here are two. In a letter to *Mother Earth*, the journal of the Soil Association (Spring 1949), Mrs. Mann writes: 'I cultivate on compost lines, but also attempt to go a stage further and use the Steiner Bio-Dynamic methods. As one result, we have succeeded in reproducing, by five years' efforts, tomato seed which retains disease resistance even if planted among other tomato plants attacked by red spider, mildew, etc. I have also received excellent report from growers concerning stamina, quality and quantity of crop. I think the main point of interest here is that the quality of our seed was developed without selection or hybridization, and thus resulted from environmental influences alone; and these were transmitted through the seed, not necessarily as a result of treatment given to the plants it produced. I had reports from people who had used neither compost, nor any organics for that matter. They had houses that were riddled with tomato diseases, yet my seed produced healthy plants. This rather confirms my view that a healthy plant has active selective capacity, which our methods of cultivation and selection tend to suppress.

"This shows that stamina, built up through the integration of living soil and seed for several generations, can overcome adverse environmental conditions, at any rate for one generation.

"My next example illustrates the same rule in the opposite sense. On the Soil Association stand at the Royal Show in 1949 we had several growing plots. One of them was barley. The bed was divided into three, the two outside plots were both composted and the center plot received nothing. Half the bed was sown with barley grown for five generations on the organic section of the Haughley

Research Farms, and the other half with barley of the same original stock, but grown for five generations on the chemical section of the farm. The line of demarcation between these two lots of seed came in the middle of the untreated plot.

"The bed was deturfed on April 8 and the barley was sown on April 9. Acute drought conditions set in immediately afterwards and a serious wireworm attack followed. When I saw the beans in May, I was doubtful if there would be a crop at all by July, but at my next visit at the end of June, this is what I saw:—

"At the half way division, clear through the middle of the untreated part of the bed, one could see, to a line, where the compost-grown seed stopped and the chemically-grown seed started. Not only was the former taller and generally more robust, but it had, in large measure, thrown off the wireworm attack— whereas the chemically-grown seed had succumbed to an extent of over 50% of the plants, even on the composted plot. By the time the Royal Show opened, the contrast was even more marked.

"Here, once again, were seed and soil operating together in the previous life history of the plant. Well composted soil could not, by itself, in one generation, enable the crop, raised for five generations on devitalized soil, to withstand the wireworm attack, while the crop from the same original seed, raised for five generations on a vital soil did so, even on the untreated plot.

"One of our visitors to the Royal Show, after seeing this demonstration, told me the following story:

"There were two fields near to each other, one had been treated organically for some time and the other chemically. The crop on the chemically treated field suffered very badly from a wireworm attack. A count was taken and the wireworms in this field were found to be two million to the acre. A count was then taken in the neighboring organically treated field, where no signs of wireworm damage was visible. Here the count was no less than five million to the acre!

"It is thus not the presence of the pest or disease organism that matters, so much as the vitality of soil, plant and animal.

"We have thought too long in terms of destruction as the only remedy for the ills that beset us. Kill, burn, or poison is the advice we get, more often than not, if we seek it in official circles. It is the advice of despair. Let us try, for a change, the constructive approach, and endeavor to build vitality and natural resistance through the operation of the nutrition cycle. It will get us further."

This report introduces a very valuable concept, that of the cycle of life, not only in terms of material elements as conventional ecology recognizes, but also a cycle and recycling of vitality or life-force. Dr. John Diamond in his fascinating book *Your Body Doesn't Lie*, described a system for testing whether various objects and substances have a strengthening or weakening effect on the human system. And everything in our environment, whether natural or artificial, does have either a strengthening or weakening influence on us; Dr. Diamond found that natural influences generally have a strengthening effect while artificial influences generally have a weakening effect, though not always. If we are sensible, then of course we will want to eat and drink only those things which have a strengthening influence; we will want to see art and hear music that has a strengthening influence, associate with people who have such a strengthening influence, etc., so that all the influences in our lives promote our growth and evolution. In other words, we will create an upward spiral of life and evolution.

But the horrible trend of modern life has been to create, in all ways, a downward spiral of degeneration that becomes a self-reinforcing system that continually engulfs more of the world and more of our lives. People eat cooked food which depresses and irritates them thus leading to a depressed and angry emotional atmosphere. No longer feeling a unity with nature, people construct the debilitating artificial environments of towns and cities in which they come to spend more and more of their lives. People subjected all their lives to all these degenerative influences create ugly music and art which further add weakening influences; they create a destructive technology which further poisons the environment with chemical and radioactive pollution, and so on, and it all adds up to an ever-more-powerful vicious downward spiral of degeneration which has now absorbed the entire human race everywhere in the world. And people who still have some of their intelligence left, are trying to fight this vicious downward spiral in all sorts of ways and in all its manifestations; some are fighting the increasingly tyranical government, some are fighting pollution, some try to fight various symptoms of the overall problem of mass degeneration, such as alcoholism, drug addiction, child abuse, crime, widespread abortions, rape, etc., etc., etc., all the various causes in which people enlist themselves in order to fight one or another of the myriad of symptoms of the general overall degeneration of the human race.

Obviously the most effective way to right the situation would be to identify the root causes of the problem and set those right, rather than try to deal with each symptom and never get at the root cause. Remember the old Greek myth about the Hydra: when one of its nine heads was hacked off, two more would grow in its place. that is how it is when we try to deal with problems without getting rid of their root causes. For instance, in trying to fight crime, people pass laws, create more government agencies and hire more cops. Since they haven't addressed the root causes of crime, the net result is that there is more crime, a bigger and more tyrannical government restricting everyone's liberties and higher taxes to pay for it.

So what are the root causes of the horrors of the modern world? They have to be something deeper than merely a flaw in the organization of the system—deeper than something like Capitalism, or Communism, or lack of education, or people not reading the Bible, or the money system. It must be some basically negative, basically anti-life and degenerative influence that is built into the very fabric of our common way of life. Various people have discovered various ways in which human life-force and human consciousness can and do become polluted with dark, stagnant, negative anti-life energy, or "DOR," deadly orgone, as Dr. Wilhelm Reich named it. Dead food, cooked food, can contribute to this pollution of consciousness, as can blocked or stagnated emotional energies. There may be other causes, but I think these two are the major, most widespread ones, cooked food poisoning being the most universal and widespread of all. Just look, in popular culture, at the tremendous prevalence and popularity of horror movies, monster movies, stories and pictures of crime and destruction—how people seem to be utterly fascinated with the bizarre, the morbid, the horrible and terrifying, and have a sort of sneering contempt for what is normal, natural, healthy and beautiful, as if it is maybe nice and pleasant, but not really important. Bizarre, morbid and horrible things are what is really serious, mature and important! But the normal, natural, healthy and beautiful are the really strong things, the bedrock and foundation of the universe that give evil and horror a stage to strut around on. I suspect that efforts to clean up the pollution and destruction of the natural world will not succeed very well until significant progress has been made in cleaning up the widespread pollution of human consciousness and human life-force, because that is the root of it all.

To get back to objective evidence for the harmfulness of cooked food in *Survival into the 21st Century*, Viktoras Kulvinskas cites a number of studies. For instance, the findings of Franz J. Ingelfinger, M.D., that hot and highly seasoned foods destroy enzymes and destroy the stomach lining, making it impossible to absorb the benefits of food. He writes:

> "Dr. James B. Sumner, a 1946 Nobel Prize winner, claims that middle-aged feeling is due to diminished enzymes as you add years to your life. Raw foods contain health-giving rejuvenating enzymes. Cooking, pasteurization, smoking, pickling, air pollution, pesticides, drugs, antibiotics, chlorination and fluoridation of water and many other interferences in nature's processes will denature enzymes, thus making the nutrients in food not readily available. These were the conclusions drawn by Jonathan Foreman, M.D." (from *Survival into the 21st Century*, by Viktoras Kulvinskas and Richard Tarca, Jr., 21st Century Publications, P.O. Box 64, Woodstock Valley, CT 06282).

A number of writers have, in fact, pounced on the enzyme factor as *the* proof that raw food is better for us. As you know, an enzyme is a catalyst, and furthermore it is an organic catalyst and a very complex protein molecule. A catalyst as you know is a chemical that makes other chemicals react with each other, while remaining unchanged itself. As organic catalysts, the enzymes are said to be absolutely necessary in order to facilitate all the myriad chemical reactions which keep the human body alive and ticking. And as complex protein molecules, these enzymes are thus said to be easily and irreparably damaged by temperatures not too much above body temperature; in fact some people are said to die from a high fever because their enzymes have been cooked by their own abnormal body heat. Now raw foods, they say, contain their own enzymes to help us digest them, but when cooked, we have to supply all the enzymes from our own inner resources and consequently we strain ourselves and wear ourselves out prematurely in trying to digest cooked food. And so this matter of the enzymes has been pounced on by a number of writers as the scientific explanation for why we do better on raw food, and they're right, but I'm convinced there are even more basic factors involved having to do with life-force.

My experience has convinced me that cooking converts the life-force or orgone energy in foods to what Dr. Reich called DOR or deadly orgone energy, a stagnant and inimical form of energy which Reich said created a desert when it was present in abnormally high concentrations in the atmosphere of an area. You see, as an artist, when I ate cooked foods I painted bleak, grotesque surrealist-type pictures with drab and dull, muddy colors; I was a creator of deserts in my art, but when I became a raw food eater, all of a sudden I began to paint instead, vibrantly alive pictures with lush abundance of healthy shapes and brilliantly beautiful colors, like the sort of lush jungle growth that Reich said was created by a strong concentration of healthy orgone energy in the atmosphere of an area.

So those raw foodists who are shy about sticking their necks out past the line of respectability drawn by the technocratic, materialistic scientists can go on talking about enzymes, but I am convinced myself that it is the corruption of the life-force in cooked foods, changing it into deadly orgone, that is the foremost reason why cooked food is bad for us. Now I expect that even, or especially the Reichians, will not like what I say here, because Reich himself never said anything against cooked food, and who the devil does a little nobody like Joe Alexander think he is to claim to know something that the great Wilhelm Reich didn't know? Well, Reich was a great genius, but he was more interested in other things and never really investigated food and diet.

But I am convinced by my experience that cooking does indeed convert the orgone energy of foods to DOR, deadly orgone, and so I'm going to say so, and furthermore I'm going to say that this is a tremendously important discovery that all people of intelligence and good will should pay attention to.

Since this is my book, I'm going to say so, though I know that people will pay no attention, and I'm sure not big enough to force them to take any notice of what I say. See, in this world, people are not looking for truth or beauty and will not pay any attention to anyone who offers them these things. People care about what you say if you are big enough to scare them. So since I'm not big enough to scare anyone, nobody cares what I say; but since this is my book, I will say it anyway. So this is my contribution, my little bit, my personal discovery, towards filling in the map of the great continent of Orgonomy that Dr. Reich proclaimed himself the discoverer of, and expected others to exlore further.

Cooking food kills the life-force in it, changes it to DOR, and raw food diet has great potential to enhance the beauty and vitality of human culture. Especially painting, the cultural activity I am chiefly concerned with, has suffered greatly because all the artists are DOR-poisoned, and this makes their colors dark and drab and weak, and it has also made many painters obsessed with bizarre and morbid subjects rather than healthy and beautiful ones. So I hope more painters will take up raw food diet because I'd like to see some more REAL painting in the world.

UNSCIENTIFIC, SUBJECTIVE & ANECDOTAL EVIDENCE FOR RAW FOOD DIET

5

WHILE IT'S NICE if you can get objective and scientific evidence in favor of the things you believe in, the only thing that really matters concerning a subject such as diet, is whether the diet in question will actually make us *feel* healthier and happier.

So let's see what some raw foodists have described as their subjective reaction to the raw food diet. First I'll give you a few that I have borrowed from other books and then some original, never-before published stories.

Prof. Arnold Ehret wrote in *Mucusless Diet Healing System:*

"If your blood 'stock' is formed from eating the foods I teach (fruits and green-leaf vegetables), your brain will function in a manner that will surprise you. Your former life will take on the appearance of a dream, and for the first time in your existence your consciousness awakens to a real-self-consciousness.

"Your mind, your thinking, your ideals, your aspirations and your philosophy changes fundamentally in such a way as to beggar description.

"Your soul will shout for joy and triumph over all misery of life, leaving it all behind you. For the first time you will feel a vibration of vitality through your body (like a slight electric current) that shakes you delightfully."

From Fred Hirsch, publisher of the Ehret books: "The complete and thorough cleansing of the intestinal tract brings an unexpected inflow of physical and mental strength. This astonishing truth that strength actually results from internal cleanliness rather than from food now hopefully dawns upon the sufferer who slowly begins to admit that eating excessive quantities of food clogs and weakens the body—dulls and depresses the mind."

Teresa Mitchell described her experience in following Arnold Ehret's teachings in Roads to Health and Happiness:

"My residence was close to the restaurant so that I could walk to and from work. There was an exceptionally steep hill which would invariably cause me to puff and pant. One afternoon on my way home I felt inspired to create a poem. As the sentences took form I became deeply engrossed in thought, when suddenly, I noticed that I had climbed more than halfway up the hill, yet I had felt no exertion whatever. It was as though I had been walking on level ground and I could scarcely believe what was happening. I concluded that I must have been so engrossed in the poem that I forgot about my body. This, then, was an opportune time to make a test, so I decided to return to the bottom of the hill and walk up again, this time giving no thought to the poem. What I discovered was unbelievable. It felt as though my body had no weight at all. Here was I, ascending this steep incline which is in all probability at least a sixty percent grade, without the slightest feeling of fatigue whatsoever. I am sure that I could have easily run all the way up, and I would have tried it too, except that I feared I would cause consternation among the puffing and panting pedestrians. It was difficult for me to restrain myself from stopping my fellow pedestrians and telling them all about it. 'I must be at the very gates of Shangri-La!' I thought to myself. 'To think that diet could do all this!' "

Dr. O.L.M. Abramowski writes in Fruitarian Diet and Physical Rejuvenation,

"The greatest change of the whole life of man and of all conditions and aspirations of his nature came with the discovery of fire. Fire is undoubtedly the greatest factor in human progress; without it the advances and blessings of civilization are absolutely impossible. If man had been satisfied to use the fire for productive and scientific purposes only, he would have become master of the earth without degrading himself to the slave of his most brutal passions and desires . . .

". . . The taste of cooked food, once acquired, has proved the curse and the bane of mankind ever since. With the help of fire, man has been enabled to render edible things altogether foreign to his digestive apparatus . . .

". . . Man found that on the artificially prepared food he grew fat and heavy, and thought he was getting strong. His desires and passions were roused through the stimulating qualities of the unnatural food, and he took that for an expression of increased vitality and vigor. His thirst increased inordinately by the artificially seasoned and salted diets; he invented fermented and distilled drinks, and mistook their baneful influence in driving the functions of the body into mad fury for a sign of increased strength and power to enjoy life. As the years went by, man became more and more short-lived, and more and more subject to disease and ailments."

A letter by a Mr. Hal A. Skinner to the "American Vegetarian" magazine, and reprinted in Morris Krok's *Fruit, the Food and Medicine for Man*, is one of the most moving testaments I have ever seen:

"I am an Australian, a descendant of the earliest British free settlers. I am an old man, recently made young again. Several years ago, I was in a very bad state of health; I read some of Arnold Ehret's works. I began the mucusless diet, developing from that to an increasingly stricter fruitarian diet, and now thriving on fruit and water exclusively.

"I do heavy work without weariness or exhaustion. My work in the desert demands endurance and fortitude for conditions are hard. Associates and others look upon me as uncanny. As far as I know, there is no other person on Earth who lives on fruit and water alone. This is not the age for such austerities. All wise persons look upon me as a fool, or a fanatic, or mad. That is part of the price a person has to pay.

"My body does not crave protein food or stimulants and evidently is perfectly nourished on fruit alone, even if the fruit is not of the best quality.

"I do not live a life of ease but am a poor man, a desert dweller. Sometimes for months at a time I am in the saddle day and night except for an hour or two of sleep I may snatch lying on the ground beside my horse. The horse is often an obstreperous animal, wild, only half-broken and ready to spring on at an instant and ride to stop my stampeding herd. I am a master drover and most of my men are unreliable black fellows. My route is across trackless regions where an accident can easily bring disaster.

"A few years ago I had to give up my work and go back to the coast, to die of disease I thought, and all who knew me thought the same. But now I am back among my beloved horses, cattle, and trackless deserts, more supple, energetic and fresh than I was when a lad . . .

". . . The discovery that there is something better in life than eating and something infinitely better than the cravings, passions, lusts, frustrations, etc. that devastate and ruin the soul through wrong eating, is to me an astonishing revelation of the first magnitude. While I am a lonesome, solitary person, I am at the same time possessor of comfort, peace, unspeakable joy and all the precious benefits that come when one of God's human creatures returns to the biologically correct diet the Great Designer and Maker arranged."

And now a section of a speech by Dr. Barbara Moore, again reprinted in *Fruit, The Food and Medicine for Man*:

"Through experimenting on myself I have found that neither energy nor heat of the body comes from food. It is an astonishing fact, perhaps paradoxical, but nevertheless quite true, that I spent three months in the mountains of Switzerland and Italy eating nothing but snow and drinking only snow water. I was climbing high mountains every day, not just fasting and sitting in a chair and reading a book or looking at the countryside. No, I was walking every day from my hotel room to the foot of the mountain, often 15 miles, climbing to at least seven or eight thousand feet, then coming down and walking another twenty miles back to my hotel.

During my extreme fasts I climbed every day, and if I could not climb on account of rain, etc., I would walk about 50 to 60 miles. Well, that conclusively proved it to me; year after year I have done the same thing just to find out whether it is true or not. Because, perhaps, one year it would work and probably the next year it would not work with the same body, I mean. So I have done it year after year and I have found it quite conclusive that energy nor heat of the body comes from food. When I found this out, I went a stage further. I decided to find out whether I could possibly live without food at all, not just for two or three months, but for a much longer period. I found that this was also possible, but not quite possible on an ordinary level, as it were. When I live in the mountains I can do that, but when I come down to 'life' it is much more difficult. The air is not the same—the tempo of life-events are not as smooth as in the mountains.

"Well, all this has made me think a lot. Eventually, of course, I hope to live entirely on air alone. That is my goal, anyhow. Meanwhile, I am now trying to circle the globe to see more people, and let people see me in order to convince them that what I have discovered is quite true. They will see for themselves that I live on an extremely concentrated diet. My diet usually consists of fruit and vegetable juices and honey, that is all—and water. I am an extremely busy person, in fact I have no time to sleep; I usually have two or three hours at the most. That is quite sufficient. I am never tired or hungry. What else can I say? That seems most important, really, not to be tired or hungry or thirsty, cold or hot, and these sensations gradually disappear. I cannot say I am impervious to most of the things that people have to fight all their lives, but gradually it becomes easier to fight them off. It is worthwhile trying to find out these things."

And from Morris Krok himself:

"As the fruitarian system is the natural way of living, it brings everything to pass, be it health, happiness or spiritual attainment.

"It was a wonderful manifestation to me that this concentrated raw regime could cure my poisoned system which had been lingering on for years. Therefore, can anyone blame me for being so jubilant about this 'superior diet' method. Remarkable also was the feeling of lightness in the abdominal navel centre; from the fact that I could now breathe deeper, it appeared that the lungs must be part of the digestive tract, or as they operate in unison, impairment in the one section will have an adverse effect upon the complementary organ."

Dr. Johnny Lovewisdom writes in *How to Grow and Eat the Vitarian Fruit-Salad Diet*:

"The volume of cooked food eaters' bellies speak for the glue, paste, and other hardened food cements deceptively attached to their enlarged bowels as nourishment for the body, which actually is a decaying mass of poisonous food waste matter clogging man's sewage system, while the fermenting contents are being absorbed for months or years, little by little along with currently eaten foods of easier absorption. Eventually one never feels well with this toxic mixture, which when eliminated on a raw food diet, makes one feel so good, as though joy effervesced from every cell in the body. It sometimes takes weeks, months, or even years to drain out all the toxins, but the reward in the happiness, fortitude and peace gained is beyond compare."

In *Natural Diet for Folks Who Eat*, Dick Gregory writes:

"As my body was cleansed of years of accumulated impurities, my mind and spiritual awareness were lifted to a new level. I felt closer to mother nature and all her children. I felt more in tune with the universal order of existence. I was now aware of the meaning of the words I used to hear in church: 'The body is the temple of the spirit.' Just as Jesus drove the money-changers out of the temple, fasting had driven the 'devils of my former diet' from my own 'temple' and my life changed completely.

"About three months after my first fast, I had a sip of scotch and soda and the taste was repugnant. That old favorite devil of mine was gone forever. I then remembered how bad liquor tastes to most people the first time they try it. Folks say you have to 'cultivate a taste' for booze. Even though the body is saying, 'No!' people repeat alcohol until they get used to it.

"With my body cleaned from fasting, I had a new hunger. I hungered to know more about nutrition and proper food so that my 'temple' would remain clean. I visited health food stores everywhere I traveled. I would head straight for the book rack and buy every book on health and nutrition I could get my hands on. I found more wisdom there than I've found on any college campus I've ever visited—and I lecture at 300 colleges a year.

"The more I read, the more I talked with Dr. Fulton and the more I experimented with my own diet, the closer I came to the fruitarian point of view concerning nutrition. After my first fast, I adopted a diet that included only raw foods. I became convinced I should leave my 'cookin' to mother nature!

"When the six basic fears (fear of poverty, fear of death, fear of sickness, fear of getting old, fear of being criticized, and fear of losing your love) disappear as a result of cleansing the system, the terrible problems rooted in these basic fears also begin to be solved—racial hatred; bigotry and misunderstanding, and infatuation with war and killing—all of the seemingly 'insoluble' problems we face."

And Arshavir Ter Havonnessian writes in a pamphlet of the Raw Vegetarian Society:

"When thousands of people all over the world, even those thought of as hopeless and incurable, have stopped taking cooked foods and medicine, they have attained real health which they have never experienced before, and thereafter need no medication of any kind.

"With all the research activity done for public health and saving the people from disease, nobody has succeeded, whereas we, the raw-eaters, have succeeded in reaching the final goal by means of natural nourishment. We are prepared at any time in any place, if necessary, to prove this undeniable fact by practical means and convince all who disbelieve."

And now here are a few original and previously unpublished stories: first one sent to me by Sherri Webb of Pasadena, California.

"My experience with raw foods began six years ago, when I accompanied a friend who had cancer to the Hippocrates Health Institute in Boston. The friend was looking for a cure and I for a vacation. After all, I was already a devout lacto-ovo-junk food vegetarian and needed no instruction in the proper way of eating.

"I had an interview with Ann Wigmore, as did my friend, as soon as we set foot in the Institute. Ann's gentleness will never be forgotten and neither will her bluntness. I learned in ten short minutes that my 160 plus pound body, acne, circles under the eyes, digestive troubles, allergies, constipation and general lethargy were far from normal. Her comments regarding the internal condition of my colon will never be put into print. My body with its wounded ego decided to give fruits, seeds, sprouts, and wheatgrass juice a two-week trial and no more.

"The 'experiment' is still taking place, and my initial negative reaction to true and radical vegetarianism has blossomed into a passion and commitment that is uncompromising. After the first year of eating about 90% raw and 10% steamed vegetables, occasional baked yams and sun baked breads, I shed 45 pounds and immediately rid myself of food, dust, and pollen allergies. In fact, I have not purchased a box of Kleenex in years. The acne faded away after two years as did circles under the eyes, which are a definite indication of renal stress and adrenal exhaustion. Constipation and lethargy go hand in hand, and both disappeared as soon as I embraced a diet of water-filled fruits and vegetables in addition to the elimination of dairy products.

"Friends would invite me to dinner from time to time and I would once again indulge in such dishes as eggplant parmesan, tofu tacos and nut cutlets with cheese. Within hours clear nasal passages became filled with mucus; indigestion reappeared as did constipation. Several of these experiences proved to me that the body is indeed a self-cleaning, self-regulatory and self-maintained organism. Foods that do not appear in nature and particularly cooked foods do the body more harm than good, because they retard the normal nourishing, cleansing and restorative process.

"The effect that raw food vegetarianism has had on mental acuity and spirituality is even more profound. A clean body and a pure mind are inseparable. After a year of proper eating, people began to praise me on writing and speaking abilities as if I were a new person. Concentration improved and an increased stamina and attention to detail became the rule rather than the exception. I require less sleep than ten years ago, and am much more productive in tasks that I undertake.

"Spiritually speaking, I feel closer to mother earth and truly connected to creation. Raw food vegetarianism is a humble way of eating. It is accepting food as it was created by God for our consumption and not trying to improve on mother nature. Raw food vegetarianism is peaceful. It is simplicity. Raw food vegetarianism is in keeping with the divine order of things. Raw foods give life rather than take it away. When the body exists in a trouble free state and the mind is pure, the soul can be free at last to express itself. The soul can play. The raw food diet is one of the most efficient ways to unite mother earth, body and mind with spirit and isn't this the purpose of living?"

The next story is from Justyn Vallori of Nevada City, California:

"In 1971 I was extremely ill. I felt that I had perhaps only one year to live. The pain was so great that I contemplated suicide.

"My difficulties were many—edema, constipation, hemorrhoids, constant back aches and migraine headaches, dizziness and faintness, losing touch with the surroundings which led to a total inability to work or cope at all in the society. I had lumps in both breasts. The lump in the right breast was so large that it protruded and looked like a small egg under my skin. The lump in the left breast was clearly and constantly visible though not as large as the lump in the right breast. There was constant drainage from both teats. The teat on my right breast began to enlarge until it was half the size of my breast. I could not even touch my breasts, they were so painful. Lying in a tub of water provided only temporary relief.

"Each month when I would menstruate, I had to stay in bed due to a great loss of blood. Standing or moving around increased the flow of blood and the pain. This condition was worsening rapidly each month.

"I think it might be of value to take you even farther back than this period, as my life-style prior to 1971 would erroneously be considered as very healthful.

"In 1960, for moral reasons, I became a vegetarian. I had previously given up the use of alcohol and cigarettes because I knew they were injurious to my health. I had stopped eating processed foods which contained chemical additives and preservatives. Most of my food came from health food stores. I took food supplements daily. I spent an hour every day practicing yoga and I did quite a bit of fasting. I was interested and was an ardent Christian Scientist for 13 years, working with affirmations, positive attitudes and metaphysical healing. My search for truth was unrelenting. I read many books and investigated diverse philosophies and religions.

"Also, I was involved in various forms of art work and music studies, as I found them of great therapeutic value on the emotional level.

"Nevertheless, in 1971, I was a physical and emotional wreck; I had black circles under my eyes that came half way down my cheeks and I was wondering how much longer I could bear the agony.

"It was at this point that a close friend of mine, who was much distressed by my situation, chanced upon a book entitled *Mucusless Diet Healing System* by Arnold Ehret. She brought me a copy which I flatly refused to read. I had read so many books on health that I despaired of finding valid information. My friend was so determined that I should read it that I finally agreed but only as a personal favor to her.

"I didn't have to read very much of it before I realized I had found the answer to my health problems. I burst into tears. I had spent my entire life searching for true knowledge and now as I stood at Death's door, my friend had handed me the key to life.

"This was in April 1971. Without hesitation, I purchased a copy of Ehret's other book, *Rational Fasting*, and set to work. Since my diet had previously consisted of almost totally cooked food, I began incorporating raw vegetable and fruit salads in my daily menu. Each morning, I sun-bathed and took enemas. I initiated many short fasts. I began deleting starches and dairy products very slowly and gradually from my diet. I also used Ehret's super mucus eliminator. I started exercising again.

"My physical condition reversed almost at once. The drainage from my breast ceased, the lumps began to slowly diminish and the right teat began to normalize in size. The menstrual problem was resolved and in every other disordered condition, improvement was obvious.

"Many of my friends were also artists and several of them offered me free dancing classes to help the healing process along. I accepted these classes with great joy. I had always loved the art of the dance but had lacked the physical health to participate.

"In the fall of 1971, I was involved in 27 hours of dancing classes a week, hours of rehearsals for a play, in addition to performing weekly with a folk dancing group of which I was the leader.

"Needless to say, in a small town like Carmel, where I was living at the time, many people were impressed by my recovery. In fact, one completely amazed man said to me, 'I don't believe it. It's as if you climbed up out of your grave onto a stage to dance.' A number of other people tried the same method with the same fantastic results.

"Today I'm still working on the transition to total raw food. My diet consists of fresh raw vegetables and their juices. Also fresh raw fruits and their juices, as well as sprouts, buckwheat lettuce, sunflower greens, dried fruits, nuts and seeds, tofu and Ezekiel 4:9 bread (a flourless bread made from sprouts). I do as much fasting as I can comfortably. I take enemas and colonic irrigations. I drink wheatgrass juice and also use it for colon implants.

"I think the most important point I would like to make to anyone interested in embarking on the transition to the raw food diet is that there should be no radical dietary changes made at any time. No long fasts until one is well into the transition and has accomplished many short preparatory fasts over an extended period of time."

The next story is from Bill Keogh of Grass Valley, California:

"My turn to a raw food diet started 20 years ago. I was beat up by a bully, and my ego was totally deflated. The first thing that came to my mind was revenge. I started lifting weights, in hopes of getting stronger than my foe. This was all the wrong reason, but having this experience of getting a black eye sprouted a seed in me that has taken me through a journey of extremes in search for perfect health and well-being.

"I went on my way for the next eleven years lifting heavy weights, getting big muscles, cramming all the food high in protein and taking endless supplements. This I thought was perfect health, although I still got sick, and I didn't feel that extremely great. I kept getting bigger until I reached 220 pounds. Being in this state doesn't do much for the betterment of the world, or inner health, mental or physical.

"As time went on I had a conversation with a wise person about eating meat. It made so much sense to me I knew I had to become a vegetarian. All my friends thought I was crazy. They said I wouldn't get enough protein and would lose my big muscles (a fate worse than death). It's not easy to become a vegetarian, or especially a raw foodist, without being around encouraging people. In my case my wife shared the same feelings. It took us eight years after becoming vegetarian to grow into raw foodists.

"It's not easy saying, 'I'm not going to eat cooked food any more.' The social pressures are tremendous, especially without understanding people to help. The rewards are great! Perfect health, a sense of well-being that can't be explained, only experienced. A deep love for the earth and its creatures. Isn't that what we can't get too much of? Love, Bill."

Tanya Keogh writes:

"Throwing away (or just not using) my kitchen stove at first seemed like a really strange idea, as it is such an intricate part of our lives. I had always been a very good cook—mostly out of necessity since my mother was such a horrid one. If I wanted to eat anything at all palatable, I had to 'cook' it myself. How was I to know that the most palatable (and nutritious) of all would have been to just not cook it at all—and anything that could not be eaten uncooked should just not be eaten. As I said, This notion of not cooking seemed very strange, but as I thought of the idea more and more it began to make a lot of sense.

"Most of my life I was quite concerned with eating properly. I have been a vegetarian for many years and have read extensively about health and nutrition. Almost all of the intelligent and well-written books on the subject advocated eating a lot of fruits, vegetables, seeds and nuts 'in the raw state if possible,' but there were few that said that everything should be raw, and if and when I did read this, somehow I just couldn't quite comprehend that this could actually be done—after all, everyone cooks. It's just something that no one questions as we (the human race) have been doing it for generations. It's just one of those rituals that everyone accepts as being very necessary—like getting a cold or two plus the flu every year, a headache at least once a week, and indigestion when one overeats (or sometimes just eats).

"Well, my husband and I were open to try new things, and quite by coincidence at the very time we were reading a book about raw foodism we met the author of the same book—our own Joe Alexander. Now reading about something and actually discussing it with an authority who has experienced it are two different things. This meeting was to change our lives. The timing was perfect as we were already interested and felt that this was just the next step in our quest for perfect health. So we took the giant step and threw away our pots and pans (our stove we kept for making tea).

"I experienced no cleansing crisis, no cold, no flu-like symptoms—just extreme energy and vitality. And I sure saved a lot of my valuable time not having to 'cook' meals. The transition was not at all difficult as I thought it might be—it was actually fun to experiment with things I had never even thought could be eaten raw—like squash, or sweet potatoes. Everything has such a unique, crispy and juicy flavor when raw. I was actually asking myself why anyone would ever want to cook those beautiful fruits and vegetables. If your kids don't like cooked peas or spinach or zucchini try giving it to them raw. Cooking takes away the sweetness, the crispness, and turns it all into a flavorless mush that needs salt, pepper, spices, ketchup, sauces or other assorted 'flavor enhancers' to make it palatable. Why go to all that trouble in the first place?

"We've been eating basically raw foods for two years now, and in that period of time I have not had one cold or flu, no constipation (or diarrhea), no infections of any kind. I've had no itching scalp, headaches, indigestion, lack of energy, irritability, insomnia, or any other affliction that people tend to think of as just a part of living.

"Animals who live on a natural diet of uncooked foods don't suffer from any of these civilized problems, so why should we? It's a lot easier than you think to become a part of nature's scheme of things. As far as I'm concerned, the only natural diet is a raw food diet."

Note from the author: I don't much like Tanya calling me an "authority" because I don't like the whole teacher-student, authority-ignoramus trip that goes on in this world; I try to write as a friend to share things I have found that make life happier for my friends out there.

Next contribution comes from Rachel of Menlo Park, California:

"*Fruitarian Times*
"Dear Everyone,
"This is my first newsletter contained in this book. Fruitarians love newsletters as they are very elfish people and love to have good fruity news. The newness of fruit diet is directly responsible for our new knowledge and healing. We love the feeling of healing. When our cells are perfect resonating crystal reflectors, perfect in shape and resonating in their own harmony, singing of the happiness of perfection, then we become as we were meant to be, as spirit-matter stars, instruments circle wheels, ourselves. Fruit fasts have been known to save all cancers. Even a live-food fast cures cancer. I can seriously say this true. This is a channeling of space-star forces and especially Luna. If you think I'm not telling the truth, then consider this fiction, total fiction, then. Belief is felt deep within and all about. So you believe what you see as a star and follow it. I see stars all around and in blue eyes especially. Singing in healing of live foods we become alkaline—the calm meditational state, and from the stillness, the calm and the harmony, the sweetness, we drink only live foods to fast and our temples are cleaned, and no longer are our intestines foul and poisoned like a garbage dump, but clean and laughing in cleanness. Our muscles can talk to each other as the neural receptors function at far greater speeds as when we drink coffee or take love. Our brain works quickly and the circuit between the brain and the source of electricity is complete as there is not a decaying, warring tie-up in the 'Middle East,' the mid-section. Our brains have electricity and our electricity has a God damn brain (damn only means 'stop' as I spelled it, you little censors.) God stop all wars caused by poisonous gases formed from decayed food in our temples—our bodies. The electricity and intelligence flows freely then through us as in a child; our wounds heal quickly and are prevented.

"Our bodies are then beautiful and clean as statues and artworks; when we advance genetic technology, we will also be able to combine these two efforts to make even a 70 year old young in 5-10 years as a 25 year old and live 500 years or so.

"There will be peace and we will all be our true child-dream selfs (elves). Never sick or poisoned from within. I quote a great spirit who said 'our blood streams are our most important rivers.' And your blood is fed by your intestines and lungs. Poisonous combinations live in the garbage of your intestines soon (10 min.) poisons your brain. DNA and RNA cannot communicate and they are *literally* drowned in sludge. They can't help. But *clean the blood* and they can help. If you see poison in your brothers, don't pour more poison on them by beating them or hurting them or putting them down. Raise them to see their own goodness that they may behold their goodness and breathe in love rather than breaths of poison from you. Love your brothers and sisters. Especially Michael Jackson, Diana Ross, the Beatles, Earth, Wind & Fire, and the Bee Gees and everyone who sings about, yes, *love.* 'Smile on your brothers everybody get together we've got to love one another right now.' My writing is all fiction and not intended to be medical advice. To God my words are all fiction and crap. This is all fiction and not medical advice. And I advise you to add to your visualization the truth of a shining star. Send for delicious recipes of live food—all quite fictional!

"Mister Spinach and Madame La Strawberry love you as much as they love the heart of Fred Astaire. As I stare into the stars, I become hysterically aware of the history of all the stories of healing from live foods. Unity is possible with love. The hope of love keeps peace.

"Raw is war turned around, live foods. You all know that if you have pain within, you will cause pain without and to all around you. Inner turmoil causes arms to follow the center, always. The center of the wheel must be peaceful. True love can make you almost peaceful with a bad diet. A good diet will be live foods and increases brain capacity, foot capacity, love capacity. A capital pacifier.

"Electricity must be harmonious to help."

And the next story is from Arbor Buchanan of Eureka Springs, Arkansas.

"For one year I have been eating a predominantly raw food diet. The most obvious change I have experienced is a feeling of unlimited energy resources, so that, in the office, where I spend eight hours a day, I often want to turn cartwheels down the halls. This also reflects my state of mind, which has changed appreciably and for the better, needless to say.

"The way I manage a raw food diet is, for the most part, to simply eat whatever is in season. Last year when I started I began with apples but soon found that too many apples gave me an odd little headache such as I had never experienced before. I switched to grapefruit and oranges, and I'd eat five grapefruits a day and oranges for dessert and snacks. Sometimes I'd have a salad. When the grapefruits and oranges ran out of their season, I switched to greens and mushrooms—I ate a lot of mushrooms. Still later in the year I ate nectarines, plums and peaches, but found that too many nectarines gave me another peculiar headache, as I had experienced with apples, only this was definitely a *nectarine* headache. I found that by eating a mono diet, I was relating to the food plant very thoroughly, coming to appreciate and love that plant food and its many facets. And so as an additional bonus, now that I begin my second raw year, I know what's on the menu for the next twelve months, and I look forward to it all.

"Physically I also feel lighter inside and cleaner and much more aware of bodily mechanisms. I have dropped twenty pounds of apparently excess weight, and while I didn't think I needed to lose before (weighed 125 at the start) obviously it was not necessary to my physical functions to have that extra twenty pounds. I feel I *need* less food, probably because the food I do eat is alive with all its energy intact."

Now a story from Darlene Evans, from Illinois:

"From spring 1980 to fall 1981, I have lived on a diet of uncooked fruit. Mentally, physically, emotionally, and spiritually I feel better than I did at ten and that was 32 years ago.

"Inspired by Kristen Nolfi, the Danish doctor who cured her own cancer with an all raw diet, I thought, why wait until I have cancer? If an all raw diet will prevent cancer, why not go on it now? It took me a full year to break away from the habit of eating cooked food.

"I could go for three weeks without a bit of fried food, and then the smell of garlic bread would get to me, and I would dive into the spaghetti dinner my daugher had made. As long as I had fallen off the wagon, I would indulge myself for the next few nights with chili and corn chips and whatever else I had craved most. Breakfast and lunch were still fruit only.

"Even while bingeing, I knew that I would try again to stay all raw. The advantages to eating fruit were heavenly: no bad breath, no body odor, no foul-smelling gas, no cooking and no dishes to wash.

"My love of dates kept me from perishing in the cold. To maintain body temperature, 10% of the diet in summer to 40% in the winter should be dried fruit.

"The cravings for cooked foods began to follow a pattern. They manifested always just before a menstrual period. In the late 1960s, my sister-in-law had loaned me a book on the all raw diet (I can't recall the title or the author, but he took long walks with only a sack of cherries). The book claimed that women on an all raw diet did not menstruate. I didn't even give it a 2% credibility. However, more than a decade later, several authors (Kulvinskas, Harris, and MacDonald) were claiming the same thing.

"When I launched into the all raw diet, my next period was eleven days late and the flow was half what it used to be. The following period was sixteen days overdue and a fourth of the usual flow. A few days of bingeing on cooked food would bring back a 28 day cycle, but with shorter and shorter binges, the flow decreased to a tenth and then only a spot. Once I realized that the cravings were occurring just before a period, I was determined to make it through this critical time.

"In April 1983, an emotional upset had me eating cooked food for several days; the period that followed in May lasted 6 days and was half the quantity of former years, convincing me that it is cooked food that causes women to bleed. I stayed fruitarian after that and haven't had so much as a spot of bleeding in six months.

"Muhammed said in the Qur'an that in heaven women would not have their courses and they would eat luscious fruit. He was giving us a recipe for heaven on earth. Women on a fruitarian diet are capable of having children who are geniuses on the average. (See Bernard)

"As 'man doth not live by bread alone, but by every word that proceedeth out of the mouth of God,' a lot of spiritual reading helps during the transition stage. I must have read a dozen Baha'i books while my diet evolved. I was elated to read that according to Abdul-Baha, in the future men will not eat meat.

"Bibliography:

"Kristen Nolfi, The Miracles of Living Foods, Life Science Publishers.

"Viktoras Kulvinskas, Survival Into The 21st Century, Omangod Press.

"Wendy Harris and Nadine Forrest MacDonald, Is Menstruation Necessary?, Life Science Publishers.

"Dr. Raymond Bernard, The Mysteries of Human Reproduction, Omangod Press.

"Julia M. Grundy, Ten Days in the Light of Akka, Baha'i Publishing Trust."

And now to go out with a bang, a final story from Sarah Bynum of Fayetteville, Arkansas:

"I am writing this especially to pregnant women new to raw food eating. May you be assured your unborn child grows well on your raw food diet.

"Years before my little girl, Autumn, was born, I began preparing for motherhood by focusing in on my diet and changing the way I was eating. I read, experimented, and listened to my body's responses and found I preferred natural, organic, whole foods; simple eating with mindful, or rather heartful attunement to source and purpose as I embarked upon eating.

"Evidence grew that eating food raw, rather than cooked, allows access to greater life energy. Furthermore, raw food could not cause damage associated with eating cooked food. For instance, my husband Paul and I would tend to eat a lot, gain weight, and yet never feel satiated (just stuffed) from cooked food; yet smaller quantities of raw food would satisfy us by meeting our nutrient/energy needs.

"During the year before Autumn's birth, my husband kept a diary as he began eating only raw foods. He recorded many positive changes such as increased stamina. He also experienced a new brighteness of outlook and disposition.

"Autumn was conceived while Paul was fasting. We naturally wanted our child to have the best possible foundation for her long life. Although raw food was the most vital food, I was yet haunted with concern for meeting 'nutritional needs' of child and mother during pregnancy—in particular protein, calcium and vitamin D. Also I had read often that a vegetarian must supplement one's diet with B12. I did not want to 'supplement' a vital raw diet. Instead, I found raw food sources of B12—alfalfa sprouts, and sea vegetables.

"Alfalfa sprouts also have vitamin D, as do sunflower seeds and dried apricots. Daily I did Tai Chi outdoors and thus got vitamin D from exposure to the atmosphere. But I relied more and more on food sources when our record hot summer made going out in the sun unbearable.

"Although I worried for my child's well-being since I had no precedent to follow, I made a leap of faith and ate nothing but raw food from the third month of pregnancy until months after Autumn was born.

"Daily I ate two tablespoons each of peanuts, almonds (or almond butter), sesame seeds (or sesame butter), pumpkin seeds, sunflower seeds, and dried coconut. Coconut has an essential amino acid often missing or proportionately less present in other protein sources. This combination of nuts and seeds provided enough protein, iron and calcium for both me and the child growing in my womb. Sometimes I snacked on these mixed together. Sometimes I rolled them into 'candy' balls using almond or sesame butter as a binder. Sometimes I soaked them in apple juice letting them swell before spoon eating them. And sometimes I added warm water and blended them for a creamy 'cereal'.

"My daily routine was one such portion of seeds and nuts, one fruit meal, and one big vegetable salad meal and fresh spring water. I was never so healthy in my life. My doctor, who normally recommended vitamin/mineral supplements to pregnant women, reviewed my diet and said I did not need supplements.

"My husband Paul and others have lost weight when eating raw food. Once a raw foodist trims down to his or her essential healthy self, his or her weight levels off, with no more weight loss. Because I was somewhat overweight when I began eating raw food exclusively, I gained only one pound in pregnancy. The excess weight that would have been lost was countered by the growth of the child in my womb. Our baby was born quickly, weight 5 pounds 12 ounces and was beautifully healthy. My milk came in abundant, good quality and Autumn grew in good health.

"My main worry throughout pregnancy was about getting enough protein. The tests kept showing a slight deficiency. The evening the midwives came to help birth Autumn, one of them entered the door telling me not to worry; they had found out that the commonly used protein test did not read correctly when the mother was alkaline, as would be the case when she ate only raw food.

"My message to you women is: raw food makes beautiful babies."

Footnote from the author: I saw this baby, Autumn, soon after she was born. I was impressed with her alertness and the appearance of interest in the world around her that she took; she struck me as appearing more alert and less drowsy than most babies I have seen.

Now one more story I want to mention. Vera Stanley Alder is the author of a fascinating book called *From the Mundane to the Magnificent*. The highlight of this book consists of the story of journeys taken, via astral projection, in the company of her guide and teacher, a man called Raphael. Raphael, it turned out, appeared the same as he did some 200 years ago, according to a past-life memory which Vera was aided in recalling by Raphael. Apparently Raphael knew secrets of greatly prolonged lifespan. Vera and Raphael explored creation from the sub-atomic level to the cellular level, from the human to the planetary, solar system and galactic, and saw that essentially the same structures and principles operated in each realm. Raphael claimed knowledge of the overall plan for human development, and of the factors responsible for humanity's present departure from this plan, so as to cause much unnecessary suffering. One quote from Raphael will show his wisdom: "It takes incompetence in all walks of life to produce such a world as we have now!" This in reference to the intellectual "specialists" in all the various professions. I was very interested to see that Raphael's opinion was that the main reason human mentality has degenerated, become weak and muddled and unable to perceive the truth, was poisoning from unnatural food! At one point he showed Vera his vision of how humans will hopefully and supposedly live in the future, when they have returned to a proper course of evolution. They had a source of unlimited, non-polluting electric power. They had reforested the world with fruit and nut trees, and took great enjoyment in tending to these trees and to their vegetable gardens. A high degree of very fine artisanry and craftsmanship was practiced in the production of goods. And they lived on fruits, nuts, vegetables and sprouted grains, all uncooked.

I know a lot of new-age people reading this book may not get the message at all. They read and think, "Oh how wonderful, in the future golden age people will live on fresh fruits and vegetables and nuts and have fruit trees all over," and meanwhile go on eating junk food themselves as if their personal actions have nothing to do with creating the future. See, people on this planet are used to thinking in terms of bosses and governments doing everything, so they're waiting for a Big Boss or a government to bring in the Golden Age. The Christians think that Jesus is going to return as a Big Boss and impose Heaven on Earth on all of us. But it's not going to happen like that at all. The New Age or Golden Age can only come when significant numbers of people decide they're going to discipline themselves to live in such a way as to continually become more and more enlightened. There is no God, no Christ, no Master or Avatar or any such thing who is going to bring in the New Age. One of the main reasons for the present mess is that everyone is looking to some leader to fix things up. But the New Age can only come if and when people quit looking for some leader to do it and take responsibility themselves for doing whatever they see needs to and ought to be done.

6 MY OWN STORY

MY FIRST INTRODUCTION TO RAW-FOODIST type ideas came in 1971 when I renewed acquaintance with a friend from high school whom I hadn't seen for several years. He had been practicing Yoga from correspondence lessons and was a remarkably transformed man; in high school I had known him as an ordinary fool, repeating the same things that everyone else said; now there was a soul looking out from behind his eyes and he spoke from an inner source of wisdom. We got to talking, and in the course of the conversation he mentioned Arnold Ehret and the mucusless diet. He said that he didn't eat breakfast any more, and told me that dairy products were unhealthful because they created a lot of mucus in the system. Well, these sounded like pretty bizarre ideas to me, because I had heard all my life that "breakfast is the most important meal of the day" as well as that dairy products were extremely nutritious and healthy foods. So I didn't pay much attention. Meanwhile I got involved in a Yoga meditation group myself because I was so impressed by my friend's transformation.

My next exposure to Arnold Ehret's ideas came in the fall of 1973 when another member of this group loaned me a copy of *Rational Fasting.* I read it and was much impressed with Prof. Ehret's writing. From doing the yoga meditation I had learned that the marks of a wise man were forceful, clear and simple presentation of ideas that appealed to one's common sense. Ehret wrote like a wise man. He didn't deal, as had all previous diet authors of my experience, with theoretical considerations of nutritional values which should theoretically make you healthier if you followed them, but with tangible and visible matters like excess mucus in the body and moreover, he promised a real feeling of greater vitality and health rather than just a theoretical concept of better nourishment. And he wasn't the sort of sentimental vegetarian who condemned meat because it was "wrong to kill animals," but he put human health first and denounced meat-eating because it loaded one's blood with putrefying toxins which weaken the meat-eater. I had tried various "health-food" and vegetarian diets and, while theoretically I was supposed to be healthier because of them, in fact I didn't feel a bit better off. So I had formed the opinion that diet wasn't a subject worth discussing or considering because you didn't feel any better even if you did eat "health foods" or follow Vegetarianism. But reading Arnold Ehret changed that.

So I immediately began following Ehret's "mucusless transition diet," which consisted of all sorts of fruits, raw or cooked, and all vegetables except potatoes, again raw or cooked. I was one of those people who experiences a very severe cleansing crisis, which surprised me because I was rather thin and had no serious health problems. What happened was that three or four days after beginning the mucusless diet I came down with symptoms of the worst case of cold, or flu, that I had ever had in my life. I am almost 6 ft. tall and my weight dropped from 145 to 105. In spite of this loss of weight, my body felt heavy as lead and it took terrific effort to get up, walk, or do any work at all. I had terrible toothaches and constant discharge of mucus from nose and throat. Despite this condition, I did my best to carry on with my life and my work as normal, because the thing I wanted to avoid at all costs was for anyone to think I was sick and try to get me to see a doctor. I was only 21 then, but had already learned enough of human irrationality and prejudice to know that no doctor was likely to sympathize with, or even try to understand, what I was trying to do. They might even think I was crazy and have me committed!

The worst of it lasted for a month; then I no longer felt as heavy and immobile as a lead statue; I could move normally again and the toothaches and constant mucus discharges stopped. But still I was grotesquely thin, not returned to normal health at all, let alone "paradise health." This condition continued for five months; then I began constantly throughout the day to cough up green blobs of mucus. This continued for a month; then all of a sudden I felt much, much better. My body felt clean inside, and working properly for the first time in my life. I felt a strong, clean, healthy sort of hunger that I had never felt before either; in fact for the seven months of the cleansing crisis I hardly felt hungry at all and would often go for days on just a few nibbles of banana. Within a week or two my weight returned to normal, just 5 pounds under what it had been before, thus disproving any notion that my previous loss of weight was due to lack of protein on the mucusless fruit and vegetable diet. On the same diet on which I had lost weight, I now regained it, now that I was clean inside.

But still it wasn't Paradise Health; there was no improvement in my general vitality. I couldn't quite figure out the reason, but persisted in the mucusless diet, feeling that eventually greater energy would come. Then finally in October of 1976, three years after I had begun, I read Teresa Mitchell's story in *Roads to Health and Happiness*. This inspired me to try an all-raw-fruit diet and thus I learned about the magic of raw foods. Mucusless wasn't good enough; the one meal daily of cooked vegetables that I had been in the habit of eating had been keeping me from enjoying the greatest benefits of natural diet. Four days after beginning this all-raw-fruit regimen, I suddenly felt a surge of energy come welling up within me such as I had never known before. Well, not quite; it resembled the rush of energy you can get by injecting ampheta-mines into your veins except that it's clean and pure and healthy sort of energy that turns your cheeks pink, not grey. Raw food diet is a better high than marijuana or speed or LSD or cocaine or any other drug you can name, and best of all the CIA doesn't make any money on it.

So I stayed on all raw fruit for a few more days and then found that eating some raw vegetables and nuts also did not diminish this new-found energy. So it was quite clear that the magic was in the all-raw diet; that that was the key to paradise health. Just mucusless diet was not enough, if it included cooked foods, although it would allow the body to remain clean and disease-free; but to experience the real magic, it was necessary to

eat only raw foods. Well, this experience was the beginning of a
new life for me, a real life, grounded in the real world of Nature. I
have done many things for self-improvement and transformation,
have practiced several yogas and meditations and other self-help
processes and have gotten good results from all of them, some
better than others, but all good; but I feel that the raw food diet
initiated the deepest, most basic and profound transformation of
all of them, the most to return me to a basic grounding in the real
world and a natural sanity. It does not contradict anything else one
may want to do for self-improvement or enlightenment, of
course, but provides the best foundation of physical health and a
mind naturally connected to reality. It helps a person to remain
constantly aware that we do not live merely to fulfill personal
goals or fulfill a role in human society or play social games, but we
have a role to play and a purpose to serve in the overall greater life
of the Earth.

It has to do with the SOEF, the Subtle Organizing Energy
Field, that Dr. Gabriel Cousens talks about in his book, *Spiritual
Nutrition and the Rainbow Diet.* We each of us have an SOEF
around our bodies as does every creature, and of course the Earth
has her own energy field too, and the energy field of every creature
is supposed to remain attuned to the energy field of the Earth, in
the manner of a radio receiver tuned to the wavelength of a
broadcasting station. And the Earth is the broadcasting station,
and the attunement of our personal energy field with the Earth's
enables us to receive the broadcast of her desires and will so that
automatically we act so as to promote the evolution of the Earth,
and since the Earth wants the greatest possible happiness and
fulfillment for all her creatures, when we act to promote the
Earth's evolution we also promote our own greatest happiness.
Now when any creature lives in a natural sort of way, eating its
natural food, breathing fresh air, etc., this automatically keeps its
energy field attuned properly to the Earth, so all its motives and
desires are in accord with the will and desires of the Earth.

But humans have found all sorts of ways to foul up, disturb
and misalign their energy fields so that they cannot perceive the
broadcasts of the Earth with any sort of clarity any longer. People

foul up and disturb their energy fields with unnatural food, by suppressing their natural feelings and by various other means, and of course now they have developed technology to generate chemical, radioactive and electromagnetic pollution on a massive scale all over the planet, further misaligning their own energy fields as well as those of all other life forms so that the whole biosphere is becoming diseased and disintegrating. So the most urgent requirement of our time, if human and other life is to survive on the planet, is for human beings to get their energy fields back into proper attunement with the Earth so that they will see a purpose beyond personal goals and human society, and act so as to properly promote the Earth's evolution.

For all practical purposes, the Earth is our God and we need to act in harmony with her will, to be one with her will and purposes. Some religions talk and speculate about the ultimate Creator of the Universe, but that is all irrelevant and far beyond our present practical needs; for all current practical human concerns we need not concern ourselves with any God beyond the Earth. Of course it's not a matter of praying to the Earth for favors because she is already doing her best to supply everything we need in abundance. It's more like, God is threatened and needs our help! People like to think of God as a great destructive power, able to take revenge and destroy his enemies, but it's more like God is the power to create life and beauty and happiness and this power is now threatened by human greed and stupidity. Ask not what God can do for you, but what you can do for God!

Now my greatest lifelong interest has been in art, most particularly drawing and painting, and one of the most astonishing results of the raw food diet was the unexpected and striking effect it had on my abilities as an artist. My drawing became much more rhythmic; strikingly so. Before it had tended to be a tangled mess of chaotic lines, but now I felt moved to draw my lines in striking rhythmic patterns. This was of course an outgrowth or expression of a more properly and rhythmically aligned energy field. It resembled the demonstration of a magnetic field with the use of iron filings. Left to themselves, the iron filings remain scattered and chaotic. But under the influence of a magnet's energy field, they align themselves in striking rhythmic patterns. The rhythmic structure of plants, trees, insects, animals, etc. demonstrates that life must be a force akin to magnetism, which affects many other substances besides iron.

I also found myself now inspired to draw figures of healthy proportions and appearance whereas before I had always tended to draw mis-shapen, sickly figures. The sort of figures that a person habitually tends to draw, especially in uninhibited doodling when the forms come more purely from subconscious expression, show that person's self-image. A person's doodled figures will express their self-image and inner condition.

In painting, the raw food diet did wonders for my color sense. I felt that a dark cloud had been swept from my mind, revealing an inner world of brilliant and beautiful color, which I was able to express something of with paints. Many people have remarked, when they have seen the paintings I have done since becoming a raw foodist, that they have never seen such strong and beautiful color in paintings before. I seldom see anything like them in the works of other painters. Very few artists have ever been good with color. Good drawing and composition are quite common, but good color is very rare. My raw foodist paintings also have a clarity that is very seldom seen in paintings. Most paintings appear as if the artist sees the world "through a glass, darkly." Or as if reflected in a smoky mirror! That is how mine also looked when I was a cooked food eater, but now they appear as if seen through freshly washed, clear glass. And overall, my raw foodist drawings and paintings have a sense of lush and abundant life, whereas before my work was dull, dreary and desolate-looking. Raw food diet put me back in touch with nature's force of creation, the force which creates grass so abundantly in the meadow, trees so abundantly in the forest, stars so abundantly in the sky, feathers so abundantly on a bird.

Twentieth-century art has been dominated by the question, shall the artist imitate Nature, or create abstractly, non-representationally, solely from his or her inner resources. The question is absurd. We *are* Nature. The artist's creative force is the same force that creates the trees and flowers and fish and everything else. The real question is, shall we express this creative force as Nature does, in an abundant, beautiful, balanced, harmonious sort of way, or shall we express it in sick, deformed, grotesque, unbalanced and inharmonious ways. Unfortunately all too many people do the latter. The art world often presents us with all sorts of sloppy, ugly, unfinished work which poses as great art, just as our government, business and academic leaders present us with a world poisoned and polluted, where most people starve in poverty while a few own more than they can possibly ever use, where amazing technological feats such as radio and television are used to broadcast the lowest sort of infantile drivel, lies and propaganda, and they tell us that this is progress and the greatest civilization ever on Earth!

Another great change that I found had come over me, resulting from the raw food diet, was a sudden renewed interest in Nature which had become lost in my teenage and early adult years. Most of my life to that point, I had lived in very big cities, Chicago and Toronto, and had felt it to be a normal and proper way to live. I had no interest in country life and if I thought of it at all, I thought of country people as backwards and not very intelligent. I thought of gardening and farming as dull, uninteresting work. Now all of that changed dramatically. Suddenly I began to notice and seek out whatever bits of Nature I could find in the city. I began to like to walk along the railroad tracks where weeds grew wild. I found squirrels, cats, birds and dogs fascinating and stopped to watch them whenever I could. Whenever I passed a house with a good garden in the yard, I would stop to look at it. I would rather go to see a garden than a movie! I began for the first time in my life to see how ugly and unnatural the city was, and how perverted people's sense of values had become. Land in the middle of a city, all paved over with concrete so that it was utterly dead, so that nothing living could grow on it, was considered extremely valuable, worth millions of dollars an acre, whereas clean land way out in the country, able to support myriads of trees and squirrels and birds and other living things, was considered almost worthless. After a couple more years I couldn't stand the big city any more at all, and moved out.

The big story on the news nowadays is, of course, the Drug Problem. Actually it's not so much a Drug Problem as a City Problem. Government policies have forced millions of people off the farms and into the cities where, if they're lucky, they can get a boring job as a cog in the Evil Machine. So to experience some sort of thrills and joy in life, they take drugs. The only real solution to the drug problem is to get the people out of the cities and back to the country and back to natural living so they can have some real purpose, opportunity and freedom in life. This of course will not be easy because the government doesn't want people to have real purpose, opportunity and freedom and the drug-takers don't know that's what they need and will probably fight any attempt to give it to them.

Now I'll have to tell you one more part of my story. Even as a raw foodist I continued drinking coffee—at first just a very little bit, but gradually let myself get more and more addicted to it until I was drinking quite a bit. Now some friendly raw foodists have wanted to totally condemn me for this, saying I am an absolute phony, charlatan and hypocrite because Natural Hygiene condemns coffee in the strongest possible terms. Howsoever, it was not my purpose to prove to anyone that I was a perfect Natural Hygienist. My purpose was to maintain the high-energy condition that raw food diet allows, and to maintain my improved sense of color and visual rhythm for painting, and to maintain a sense of spiritual unity with Nature. Coffee didn't seem to interfere with any of these things, so I figured the dangers of it must be grossly over-rated. After all, it was only a little natural bean flavoring dissolved in water. And it was mucusless. Putting sugar in it definitely made it bad for you, but I figured the coffee itself must be relatively harmless.

So as I said, I enjoyed it very much and felt very little of any "drug effect" from it—very little stimulation. So I gradually let myself get more and more addicted to it until I was drinking quite a bit indeed. And so on one fine spring morning, after a sip of coffee, I felt the most horrible pain in my stomach, such as I had never felt before and hope never to feel again. "Sounds like an ulcer," said one friend; and so I figured that must be what I had. I got a Natural Hygienist friend from Texas to send me copies of all the articles on ulcers that Herbert Shelton had written for his *Hygienic Review.* I found I had the typical symptoms for ulcers—eating something relieved the pain; on an empty stomach the pain got worse. Shelton thought that to rest and fast was the surest way to heal an ulcer. He gave numerous examples of people who had had ulcers for years, and had taken drugs for years and lived on bland diets and in some cases even had operations, but they still had ulcers; but when they finally came to a Natural Hygienic practitioner and rested in bed and fasted a few weeks, they got all better.

Now medical doctors, and even most Naturopaths, say that a person with an ulcer absolutely should not fast. They say this because of the fact that the pain increases on an empty stomach. Shelton took a longer-term view, which made perfect sense to me. When a person with an ulcer fasts, the pain may get worse for the first two or three days, but then the stomach stops secreting the digestive acids and the pain diminishes, and with a complete rest from work, the stomach can heal itself quickly then. So even ulcers that have gone on for years, generally heal during a two to three week fast; often even sooner.

So that is what I did. First, I fasted for seven days. It probably healed up then, but I thought I still felt some pain, so I fasted another four days. Then I thought maybe I still wasn't all better, so I fasted another five days. Well, this sort of thing went on for the next year and a half. I still thought I felt some pain in my stomach and so over and over I fasted for anywhere from two days to two weeks. Several times I fasted for 10 days, several times for 7 days. It was the most fasting I have ever done, and for that reason was a valuable and interesting experience. I think I must have gotten as cleaned-out as a person can get by fasting. During the first couple of fasts, I had the typical feelings of a cleansing crisis—felt very heavy, low energy. Then after a certain point, energy came back; I felt the inner resistance had disappeared and I was free to move around about like normal. I had heard of people experiencing a return of energy on a fast, after a thorough inner detoxification, but hadn't experienced it before. My experience was that, sitting or lying down, I felt absolutely drained of energy, like I didn't want to move. But if I did force myself to get up and start moving, I soon felt quite energetic and able to run about almost as well as normally. But then, as I continued fasting more and more, even this energy became exhausted until it became an immense effort just to turn over in bed! Well, because of this I am no longer much interested in Breatharianism—that is, the idea of living only on air and water with no food. I am convinced now that my body does actually need a little food.

After about a year and a half of doing all this fasting plus trying all sorts of other natural remedies for ulcers, such as comfrey tea, comfrey-and-slippery elm tea, aloe vera, and trying various "super-food" supplements like barley green, bee pollen and Body Toddy, a man who heard of my problem came to talk to me. He asked if I had ever had the medical tests, the x-rays or the endoscope, to find out if in fact I really did have an ulcer.

No, I hadn't. I had been to one M.D. who gave me a prescription that I took for a few days and then quit because it didn't feel like it was doing me any good, but hadn't had a real thorough medical diagnosis.

So he told me his story. Twenty years ago, he had had a pain in his stomach that he thought was an ulcer. He read books on ulcers by the best medical specialists in the field. He lived on a bland diet and took antacids by the semi-load. He had x-rays which showed nothing wrong but he still had a pain in his stomach. Finally he went to a surgeon and said he wanted an operation. The surgeon said he wouldn't operate without first getting a diagnosis of the problem by an endoscope, and sent him to an endoscopist. The endoscopist examined him thoroughly, found nothing wrong and told him to go home. So he went home and a couple months later the pain disappeared. He never did know what it was.

So he advised me to get an endoscopic examination. He even pulled $200 out of his wallet and gave it to me and said that if that didn't cover the cost, to let him know! And further he gave me the name of what he thought was the best doctor in town to go to.

It was an offer I couldn't refuse, so I did it. First I had to go to this doctor for a complete check-up. He couldn't find anything wrong. So he sent me to the endoscopist. The endoscopist found a small scar in the duodenum where there used to be an ulcer but it was all healed now. He said that any pain I was still having must be muscle spasms, sort of a charley horse in the stomach; quite common but nothing to worry about, he said. And he gave me a prescription for a drug to relax any such muscle spasms. On my way home I saw a bumper sticker that said, "Just Say No to Drugs;" thought it sounded like a good idea and threw away the prescription. Been all right ever since; a little pain now and then, but I don't worry about it.

Well, it was an interesting experience, and I learned some things from it. Firstly, that coffee isn't harmless. It can definitely cause ulcers, if you drink it like a mad fiend. I still like the stuff an awful lot, and drink a little bit, but just a little bit. And I learned a lot about fasting, and how my body responds to it. As mentioned, I don't have any illusions any more that maybe I can be a Breatharian and live without any food. I also learned a lot about ulcers. The doctor I saw told me that 20% of Americans have them at some point in their lives. Can you believe it? I never would have suspected the percentage was so high; I would have guessed maybe 5%. The MDs also say they still don't know what causes ulcers. Well, it's no mystery to me any more, considering how much coffee Americans drink, and how much liquor, and corrosive soft drinks like Coca-Cola, and how much fried foods and bad food combinations people eat, that cause terrible acid indigestion. Then throw in all the worries people have, about paying their mortgages, loans, taxes, doctor bills, and insurance, and it's not much of a mystery any more. But the MD's probably want to find a virus that causes ulcers, so they can develop a drug to kill it and be heroes in the War on Viruses, and since they haven't been able to find that virus yet, they say they don't know what causes ulcers.

I learned also that the MDs overcharge like crazy; a medical doctor will often charge more for a half hour procedure than a Natural Hygienist will charge for a week's stay at a Health School. Guess which one will usually do you more good? The doctors can do it, of course, because they've got most people convinced there's no alternative and if they don't run to the doctor with every little pain or sniffle they might die! And since people eat so stupidly and live so unhealthy, they get plenty of pains and sniffles and the doctors can charge all the traffic will bear. Then, also, most people now have medical insurance, and so it's just like auto insurance, where the body shops figure "what the hell, the insurance is paying for it," and jack up the price.

I do want to give the doctors their proper due, though. There are some things the MDs are really good at. They are really good at first-aid type treatments, treatments of injuries, setting broken bones, removing bullets, stitching up wounds, emergency rescue surgery; that sort of thing. The endoscope procedure, while it didn't help me get better, was valuable in letting me know that I had gotten better. If people were smart about it, they would see that each branch of the healing arts has its area of competence, its special field where it has the best knowledge. MDs are good at first-aid, treatment of injuries, and rescue surgery. Chiropractors are good at getting your spine in proper alignment. Natural Hygienists are usually the best for prevention of disease and overcoming disease and restoring the body to optimum health. And so on. Let's just keep it straight who's good at what. Nobody but a fool would go to a Natural Hygienist for a broken leg, or to a Medical Doctor for Arthritis or Tuberculosis or other disease.

7

HOW TO
BECOME A
RAW FOODIST

NOW SOMETIMES THERE ARE PEOPLE who are attracted to raw
foodism but don't know just how to go about doing it. After all,
it's a very unaccustomed thing for most people to do. Most of us,
all our lives, have become used to eating cooked food with every
meal, to spending a substantial amount of time over at the stove
shuffling pots and pans around, turning the burners up and down,
putting in a dash of this and a pinch of that . . . it would certainly
feel strange to suddenly stop all that. It would feel eerie. Suddenly
there would be this big hole, this immense void in your life. It's
like you've been carrying around a 75 lb. backpack all your life
and now all of a sudden you're supposed to take it off. You've
been fiddling with straps and shifting the weight around and
learning to walk a little stooped over to balance the load—and
now someone is asking you all of a sudden to take off your
backpack! It would certainly feel strange to be without it. What
would you do with all the time you used to spend fiddling with the
straps and adjusting the load? And how strange it will feel not to
have that weight on your back! So you see why people find it
strange to contemplate the idea of becoming raw foodists.

Not being accustomed to raw food eating, some people create
some strange, imaginary, mystical ideas about what it is. For
instance, some people I have met, seem to think of raw food eating
as a sort of unattainable ultimate goal of life, some sort of far off
blissful, ecstatic condition that you can hope for and long for and
gradually work towards but can never quite actually attain. Well,
of course it is nothing of the sort. Raw food eating does help to

keep your emotions at a higher tone, so you don't get as far down in the dumps as you used to. But the purpose of life is not to become a raw food eater. Rather the purpose of raw food eating is to keep you healthy and energetic and clear of mind so that you can better accomplish some worthwhile goals in life.

Now when the question comes up, of how does one actually become a raw foodist, I am reminded of the old saying, "A number of possible and more-or-less equally effective modes of procedure are at the disposal of one whose chosen goal is to remove the hide from the mortal remains of a cat." Sometimes this old saying is alternatively expressed as, "Numerous possible options may be successfully employed by one who desires to accomplish the removal of the epidermal organ from a feline cadaver," thus proving that there's more than one way to skin a cat!

One way to become a raw foodist is to just go ahead and do it. For instance, one friend once told me about a man who read about raw foodism and decided right then and there that he was going to do it, and not only himself but his whole family was going to do it. So he drove to the farmers' market, loaded up the car with fruit and drove home. When he got home the kids looked at all the peaches and watermelons and bananas in the car and said, "Oh boy, dessert!" And the man answered, "Yep, kids, from now on it's all dessert!"

Some people prefer to go into it more slowly and gradually, of course, like someone who wants to go into the pool at the shallow end and test the water every inch of the way to make sure that there are no sharks or that the water is not going to suddenly turn boiling hot or something. Many transition diet plans have been developed for people who prefer this approach. For instance, Arnold Ehret developed the plan of first replacing your mucus-forming foods with mucus-lean foods. (i.e. baked potato, whole grain crackers or dry whole-grain toast, baked sweet potato, and fish) and then gradually replacing those more and more with totally mucusless foods, and thus gradually working your way towards the ideal of a raw fruit, vegetable and nut diet.

Viktoras Kulvinskas in *Survival into the 21st Century* has much good information on transition diets, as does also *Fit for Life* by Harvey and Marilyn Diamond.

I'll give you a transition diet plan here also. Some people like to have such plans. Many people are a little afraid to try to figure out what to do all on their own. They feel safer if someone else tells them what they should do. That way they feel they are under the safe guidance of an expert instead of under the dangerous guidance of their own incompetent selves. Actually it's plenty OK to experiment and work things out on your own, find what feels good for you, in this matter of natural raw food diet. In the line of raw foods, pretty much anything you eat is going to be safer than a doughnut or a hamburger. If you do make a mistake, the worst that can happen is that you get a little indigestion from a poor combination. It's hardly possible to become malnourished on a raw food diet, even if it doesn't contain a huge variety of foods. I once lived for 56 days straight on just juicy fruits, no bananas or avocadoes or vegetables. I never felt stronger in my life. The diseases of malnutrition, like scurvy and beri-beri and so forth, are quickly relieved with fresh fruits and vegetables. So I think the best thing is to experiment and eat what you like, in the quantities that feel good to you, just keeping in mind a few simple principles, i.e.: 1. Only fruit in the early morning, or no breakfast at all. 2. Don't combine fruits with vegetables or seeds at the same meal. 3. Don't combine high protein foods with starchy foods. 4. You'll feel a lot better if you don't eat late at night, less than 3 hours before sleeping. Go to bed hungry, and you'll feel more alert when you wake up.

For people that REALLY want someone to tell them just what to do, John Tobe wrote a raw food diet plan that gave a complete schedule of recipes for every meal, 365 days a year.

Now then, here is my transition diet plan. Remember I am not an expert or authority and I do not claim my plan is the best plan. It is, however, a practical and workable plan which will improve the health of a person who follows it. This plan is meant to be applied at intervals of three months; that is, do step one immediately, step two in three months, step three, three months after that, and so on.

1. Give up white sugar, white flour, white rice and any other polished grains, and give up all the carbonated soft drinks.
2. Give up any daily drinking of alcohol. Cut it down to once a week or less. Preferably none. Quit trying to drown your problems in drinking, you jerk! The world needs sober workers to spread the truth and build a better way of life. You don't help anybody by lying around like a stupid drunken pig making a fool of yourself. And if you're smarter than me, you'll quit any coffee or tea drinking at this point too.
3. Give up cooked red meats, i.e. cattle, pig, sheep, horse, goat, deer, rabbit, armadillo, moose, etc.
4. Give up cooked eggs and all pasteurized or cooked dairy products.
5. Give up cooked white meat, i.e. fish, chicken, turkey, duck, pigeon, squid, snail, oyster, snake, frog, iguana, octopus, etc.
6. Give up cooked grains, i.e. wheat, oats, corn, millet, etc.
7. Give up cooked beans, and roasted nuts.
8. Give up cooked potatoes.
9. Give up all cooked vegetables.
10. Don't even stew your prunes or bake your bananas anymore.

This is it, the 30th month, it's taken you 2½ long, tortuous, excruciating years of blood, toil, tears, sweat, pain and sorrow, but you've finally done it! You're a real raw food eater! Congratulations! Mother Earth welcomes you back into the fold of her normal, sane, sensible creatures!

Now a few of the fine points of raw food eating, over which the different factions in the overall movement sometimes bicker.

—Nuts: Some say that nuts have an enzyme inhibitor in them that makes them difficult to digest, and that you should soak your nuts in water, therefore, for 24 hours before eating them, so that the nut comes back to life and the enzyme inhibitor is deactivated, in preparation for the sprouting of your new little almond tree or hazelnut tree or whatever you've got there. The purpose of the enzyme inhibitor was to keep the nut from sprouting before conditions became right for the baby tree to grow in. Same goes for sunflower seeds and sesame seeds, of course.

—Seaweeds: Natural hygienists don't believe in seaweed. They say that humans are land animals, not Alaskan fur seals or humpback whales or some such thing, and therefore not meant to eat sea vegetation. They say we should put seaweed on our garden, to fertilize the soil, and thus get whatever nourishment the seaweed gives, second-hand, when our cabbages pick it up from the soil. Personally, I love seaweed. I put powdered kelp on salads, and occasionally use other types of seaweeds too. I don't feel like it's done me any harm so far, though senior citizens tell me I'm still young and so there's still time for all sorts of hell to break loose.

—Raw meats and fish: Most raw foodists are fanatic vegetarians and wouldn't dream of eating raw meat or fish or eggs. But, as mentioned earlier, apparently many people have lived in excellent health on raw meat or raw fish. Personally, I've got nothing against such foods, though I very, very seldom eat them. The few times I have tried them—well, did you know that fish and hamburger actually taste better raw than cooked?

—Raw dairy products: Obviously not really a natural food for any adult creature, but probably not harmful either. Adult cats seem to do quite well on raw cow's milk.

—Honey: Is raw honey OK? Some don't think so. I'm no expert on this. It seems more-or-less natural enough—if bears eat it, why not people? Apparently the pollen is very beneficial. Personally I don't eat it because I don't like it—too overpoweringly sweet; but I've got nothing really against it, except one fellow I know blames honey for ruining his teeth, just like sugar.

—*Dried fruits:* They fall in between fresh and cooked foods; they're not the best thing but not particularly harmful either. If you try to eat just dried fruits for a while, you get a terrific craving for something fresh. It's a good idea to soak dried fruits in water for a few hours, till they swell up almost like a fresh fruit again. I once read a book by a dentist who was concerned with preventing cavities. He said that if you eat dried fruits, you should eat an apple or some sort of fresh, juicy fruit right after, to clean your teeth. Bits of the dried fruits, he said, would stick to your teeth and possibly cause cavities, but eating something like an apple or orange would wash it away and clean your teeth. Sounds like a good idea to me. Nuts and seeds tend to be sticky too, so it's probably a good idea to eat some celery or cabbage leaf or cucumber, some sort of fresh juicy vegetable, after eating nuts, to clean your teeth.

Macrobiotics advocates a balance of "yin and yang" foods, foods of opposite qualities, and my experience is that when the body is well-cleaned and restored to health by fasting and raw food diet, you naturally want a certain balance of foods of opposite qualities. For instance, if you eat just juicy fruits for a while, you crave for something heavy and fatty, like avocadoes or nuts. Conversely, if you eat just nuts and avocadoes for a while, you start to crave for something sharp and juicy like citrus fruits. Dr. Johnny Lovewisdom wrote that when he tried to live just on sweet tropical fruits, he began to crave for bitter vegetables. So while I can heartily endorse this principle of a "balance of the opposites," I think one will be healthier by achieving it with natural uncooked foods, than with the cooked grains and vegetables that Macrobiotics recommends.

Macrobiotics, of course, is another philosophy that many health-and-truth seekers are attracted to; in fact many more are attracted to Macrobiotics than to raw foodism because it's a lot easier; you don't have to give up your deep-seated addictions to cooked grains and beans to do it, and because it has the aura of mysterious exotic Oriental wisdom to it which is so attractive to Westerners who are starting to mature beyond the shallow pseudo-rationality of Western technocratic materialism. Another case of seeking to balance out the opposites! And Macrobiotics does bring considerable improvement in the health of people who follow it because it's much more natural and intelligent than the common junk-food diet. As one raw-foodist friend of mine said, Macrobiotics is "the second-best diet in the world!" Macrobioticists defend cooking by saying it was perfectly natural for humans to discover the use of fire and salt in preparing food. And it's true. It was perfectly natural. And now it has become perfectly natural for some of us to discover that this fire-and-salt treatment is destructive to our health and we do well to give it up! It is natural for a child to put its hand in the fire. It then becomes natural for it to discover that it thereby gets burned, and not to do it anymore. One more point I want to congratulate the Macrobioticists on. I once saw a book, written by a Macrobiotic author, whose title I would give first prize to any day. It was, *Civilization—Its Cause and Cure.*

I have met many people who say that they would like to live on raw food if they lived in a warm climate, but it is too cold where they live. When I lived in Canada, I met such people. Then in northern California, where there is hardly any winter at all, compared to Canada, I met people who said it was too cold there to be a raw foodist. Now here in Arkansas, which, to me, coming from Canada, is like a tropical jungle, I still meet people who say it is too cold here to be a raw foodist. And when I have visited the area around Austin, Texas, which is so far south that I was able to stand outside all day painting a landscape between Christmas and New Years, I still met people who said it was too cold there to be a raw foodist which makes me wonder where these people think it is warm enough to be a raw foodist—the center of the sun maybe?.

I have never had problems being a raw food eater in cold weather. In fact, it helps me stand cold weather better. As a cooked food eater, my hands and lips used to crack and bleed when it got cold. That doesn't happen when I stay on raw food. And I have more energy to run around and be active to generate body heat. There are millions of wild animals living in Canada.

Every one of them is a 100% raw food eater. So what makes people think they are special and need cooked food? Eating raw food doesn't mean you have to eat it ice cold from the refrigerator. You can warm it up to room temperature or body temperature. Anthropologists have apparently discovered that cooking began in northern Europe, where people would put frozen foods over a fire to thaw them out. Fine. Then they got careless and left them over the fire too long, and that's when our troubles began.

Conversely, raw food diet helps me to stand extremely hot weather better, too. I once went with some friends to Tucson, Arizona, in the middle of summer. They were eating ice cream and potato chips and were always thirsty, always wanting to stop for Cokes or beer. I just had a few peaches now and then and was fine. I just don't find any natural or intrinsic disadvantages to raw food eating, only advantages. All the disadvantages come from the fact that society is designed to cater to cooked food eaters, not raw food eaters. People can accomplish anything they consider really important. As Herbert Shelton wrote, the Army has no problem making sure all the soldiers in Alaska have all the electronic equipment and ammunition they could possibly need. If society considered it important for everyone to have fresh organic fruits and vegetables so that they could be healthy and contribute their greatest potential of good work for the benefit of all, that could readily be accomplished, too.

Okay, one more thing for the people who think they need hot food in cold weather and therefore can't be raw foodists. You can do these things, I think, and still enjoy Paradise Health: Drink hot drinks in cold weather. Herbal teas, vegetable broths—for instance, you can boil some spinach and squash and such like things and pour off the broth and flavor it with some olive oil and seaweed and cayenne pepper, and drink that. My experience is that drinks consisting almost entirely of boiled water don't spoil the raw food high. Also, you can eat some cooked fruits—for instance, stewed prunes or baked bananas. Fruits seem to be so pure that even cooked they don't depress you. Still best to have them raw, but this is what people can do who want to be raw foodists but feel they just have to have some hot food in winter.

8 THE TIBETAN REJUVENATION RITES

THE TIBETAN REJUVENATION RITES are a set of five simple, easy-to perform exercises that many people have found to dramatically increase their vitality and sense of well-being.

They were first published in 1939, in a small book by Peter Kelder. Kelder had learned them from a man he called "Colonel Bradford." Colonel Bradford had been a British officer who at one point in his career was stationed in India. While there, he repeatedly heard stories from the natives of a certain district in the Himalayas, of a remote lamasery where apparently nobody ever grew old. Men of well over 100 years of age who resided there, reportedly retained the appearance, strength and vigor of healthy men of 30 to 35 years old. Further, old men who went to live at this lamasery, reportedly began to look and act dramatically younger within a few months.

After his retirement, Colonel Bradford found himself rapidly growing old, feeble and decrepit. He had to lean on a cane to walk. He remembered the stories he had heard in India. Could there possibly really be such a place as that lamasery? He determined to go back and search for it and find it if he could. He tried to persuade his friend, Peter Kelder, to accompany him on the search, but Kelder prudently refused, not wanting to disrupt his life for what was probably a wild-goose chase. So Colonel Bradford set out alone.

After many long, hard months of searching, the Colonel finally arrived at the lamasery and entered into the way of life there. Within a few weeks he began to feel surprisingly younger and stronger. Soon he was able to throw away his cane and engage in hard physical labor. He spent two years at the lamasery, then went to India for a few months to teach his new-found knowledge to others. The lamas weren't really trying to keep anything secret. But their remote location, combined with the natural skepticism and laziness of the human race, prevented their secrets of health and rejuvenation from becoming more widely known, just as the skepticism and laziness of the human race will ensure that very few people will ever benefit from this book, though it contains enough practical knowledge to eliminate 90% of the diseases people suffer from, and to remake the world into a virtual Paradise.

At the lamasery, Colonel Bradford learned many valuable keys to health and happiness, and the core of the lamas' knowledge was, apparently, the Five Rites presented here. Finally Colonel Bradford returned to New York, where he looked up his old friend Peter Kelder. Kelder at first could not recognize the Colonel. He was expecting to see a feeble old man of 70 or so and instead a vigorous man who appeared about 40 stood before him. He thought it must be Colonel Bradford's son, not the Colonel himself! Naturally, he pressed Colonel Bradford to tell him what he had learned, Colonel Bradford did so, and Kelder immediately began practicing the Five Rites, and soon found the results to be excellent. He organized classes for the Colonel to teach others, who also benefitted splendidly from practice of the Rites.

Colonel Bradford explained that, while the Rites may have a little value for promoting muscular strength and flexibility, that is not their prime purpose. I have found this also. I have done many exercises that stretch and exert the muscles, building strength and endurance, much more than do the Five Rites. However, the Five Rites have raised my overall energy and vitality much more than any of the other exercises I have done. This, as the Colonel explained, happens because of their effect on the Chakras, the seven subtle centers along the spine through which the body is connected with Spirit. In a young, vigorous, healthy person, said the Colonel, all the Chakras spin at a high rate of speed and at the same speed. As we grow older, one or more of the Chakras tends to slow down and fall out of harmony with the others. The result is that the flow of energy through the body is weakened and thrown out of balance, leading to depression, nervousness, disease and decay. Daily practice of the Five Rites soon gets all the Chakras spinning rapidly and in harmony again, often making the practitioner feel dramatically revitalized and rejuvenated. I began to really feel the results after 21 days of daily practice, and this is apparently a common experience.

Colonel Bradford recommended that one begin by practicing each Rite for 3 repetitions daily, for the first week. The second week, do each one 5 times, the third week 7 times, and so on, adding two repetitions of each Rite per week until you are doing them 21 times daily; then maintain this level of practice. If you have difficulty doing some of them, then just do the best you can without overly straining yourself; you will get benefits from whatever you are able to do; and eventually, with persistent effort, you will become able to do them all properly.

In addition to the Five Rites, Colonel Bradford taught a Sixth Rite, whose purpose is to raise the sexual energy to the higher chakras, and transmute it for the renewal of the practitioner's entire body and mind. Colonel Bradford only taught this Sixth Rite to people who had practiced the first five for at least ten weeks, and then only to those who avowed that they felt "sexually complete" and prepared to remain celibate the rest of their lives in order to transmute all their sexual energy into rejuvenation via this Sixth Rite. The reason he only taught it to persons who had practiced the first five rites for at least ten weeks, was that he was dealing mostly with impotent old men, who had to practice the Five Rites for ten weeks to regain their virility. He said it was impossible to transmute sex energy if you had none to transmute.

Being too damned curious for my own good, I have frequently practiced the Sixth Rite to find out just what it will do, though with no intentions of remaining celibate the rest of my life. Practice of the Sixth Rite does indeed send a strong current of energy up the spine and into the head, refreshing the mind and body. And it is sex energy; if you do the Sixth Rite immediately after experiencing orgasm, nothing happens; the energy that makes it work is depleted. Is it really necessary to remain totally celibate to benefit from the Sixth Rite? Obviously not; a normally healthy person has enough energy for a satisfying sex life and to get some benefit from the Sixth Rite, unless their idea of a satisfying sex life is 3 or 4 times a day every day which I strongly suspect most people would find extremely boring and tiresome. So, looking at the thing strictly from a physiological standpoint, leaving aside all questions of alleged morality and immorality, what we have is this: the sexual orgasm depletes the energy which is channeled to the higher chakras by the Sixth Rite. The energy builds back up again quite rapidly so a person would have to have a hell of a lot of orgasms to deplete all their energy so that none is ever available to raise and transmute via the Sixth Rite. The gods wanted you to have plenty of rope to hang yourself whenever you desired, so they gave you Free Will. So it's up to you to decide whether to use up your energy in having orgasms or in doing the Sixth Rite or in some other fashion altogether, and how much of each you want to do. Why do the Sixth Rite? Because it gives you more responsibilities. See, generally people are self-centered, concerned only with their little personal lives, personal problems and personal success. When you get energy into the higher chakras, you start feeling concerned and responsible for bigger things—for your community, your country, humanity, the environment, the Planet. I think they call it Cosmic Conscious-ness—feeling responsible for all humanity and all life on Earth, feeling like the problems of billions are on your shoulders, rather than just the problems of yourself and your family. So if that's what you want, go ahead and do the Sixth Rite.

Colonel Bradford recommended practicing the Sixth Rite when you feel strong sexual desire; because that's when the sex energy is at its peak. Three to four repetitions of the Sixth Rite will be enough to raise and transmute whatever sexual energy is available for this purpose at the time; you will feel it when all the available energy has been utilized.

I recently received the following comments on the Rites from Kyle Griffith, the well-known author of *Spiritual Revolution* and *War in Heaven*, the "most controversial channelled books of the 20th century." He says,

"I learned the first five of the Rites when I was a tiny kid and was told they were the fundamentals of Yoga. Well, they are, but it's Tantric Yoga, and they are excellent conditioners for the practice of any kind of Sex Magic. I still do all of them except the first quite frequently, and I think if any set of physical exercises can keep people youthful, these could do it.

"I'm enclosing ten bucks for copying and postage expenses, and would like a hundred copies of the pamphlet to circulate as a rider with the issue of TSE ("The Spiritual Revolutionary," a letterzine edited by Griffith) that discusses this subject. I assume I have your permission to just run your Rite #6 page as a page in the same issue. A number of New Agers have expressed reluctance to publish this exercise or a variant of it, because they feel it may hurt people who haven't practiced the first five Rites regularly for some time beforehand. The caution makes perfect sense, but I trust my readers to know whether they're ready for it or not.

"In order to practice the Sixth Rite during intercourse, it's necessary to omit bending at the waist in Step Two. The purpose of the bend is to unlock the ligaments at the top of the pelvic girdle that the waist locked while standing—this allows the diaphragm more play so a maximum amount of air can be forced out of the lungs. One can accomplish the same unlocking action without bending simply by arching the back slightly and then consciously unarching it. And in step three, if you're not in a position to stretch your torso by pushing down on your hips with both hands, you can stretch it by reaching your arms over your head and pulling on the bedstead.

"Like you, I think much of what the old-time Theosophists and similar occultists had to say about sexuality was puritanical nonsense. However, there's a grain of important truth in the warning about Rite #6 and celibacy—it does discharge sexual energy without orgasm, by distributing it out among the various chakras. So it can be used as an alternative to masturbation for relieving sexual frustration due to excessive practice of Karezza or some other cause. And it can also be used for solo Sex Magic by masturbating almost to orgasm and then channelling the energy with Rite #6!"

And that closes Kyle Griffith's comments on the Tibetan Rejuvenation Rites.

Should you want more information on the Rites or want to read Colonel Bradford's story for yourself, I know of two editions of Peter Kelder's book that are currently available. The full original text is available as *The Five Rites of Rejuvenation*, published by Borderland Sciences, P.O. Box 429, Garberville, California 95440. Borderland publishes it as an amateurish-looking booklet. Another version, in slick paperback form with attractive illustrations, but considerably edited and revised so that the flavor of the original is lost and some interesting parts of the story are left out, is published by Harbor Press, P.O. Box 1656, Gig Harbor, Washington 98335, under the title, *Ancient Secret of the Fountain of Youth*.

Anyone interested in Kyle Griffith's book, *War in Heaven*, or his letterzine, "The Spiritual Revolutionary," can write him at S/R Press, P.O. Box 60327, Palo Alto, California 94306.

By the way, you gan get plenty of benefit by doing the first Five Rites and not getting involved with the Sixth Rite at all.

FIRST RITE

Stand upright with arms horizontally outstretched. Then spin around clockwise, that is, in the same direction the hands of a clock would turn if it were placed face up on the floor. Spin fast enough to get a little dizzy. To keep from losing your balance, focus your eyes on a point in front of you and keep focused on it as long as you can as you begin spinning; then when you spin out of range, quickly whip your head around to re-focus on your point as soon as possible. Please note—it is not necessary to spin on your toes like a ballet dancer. You can shuffle your feet around like a clumsy hippopotamus—just get yourself spun around somehow, CLOCKWISE.

SECOND RITE

Lie on a mat or rug on the floor, arms at your sides. As you inhale deeply, raise your head to touch your chin to your chest, then raise your legs to a vertical position or even extend backward somewhat so that your feet are directly over your head. Hold this position for 2 or 3 seconds, then, exhaling, lower your legs and head to the floor again, rest as desired, and repeat.

THIRD RITE

Kneel on your mat, hands on sides of thighs. Lean your head forward to touch chin to chest, then, inhaling deeply, lean backwards as far as you can, bracing hands against thighs for support. Hold for 2 or 3 seconds, then exhale as you return to starting position. Repeat.

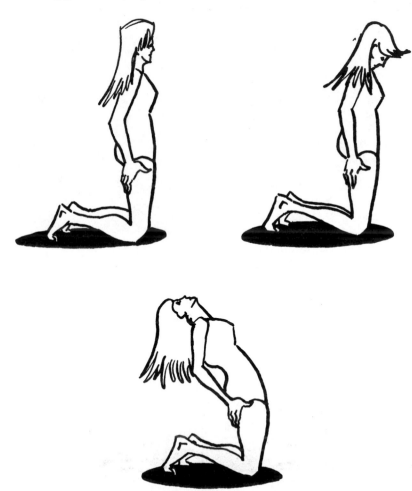

FOURTH RITE

Sit on your mat on the floor, hands beside buttocks, legs straight out in front of you. Now lean your head forward to touch chin to chest, then, inhaling deeply, lean your head back as far as possible and raise your body up on straight arms and bent knees, so your body is horizontal. Tense all muscles throughout your body briefly, then exhaling, lower yourself back to starting position and repeat.

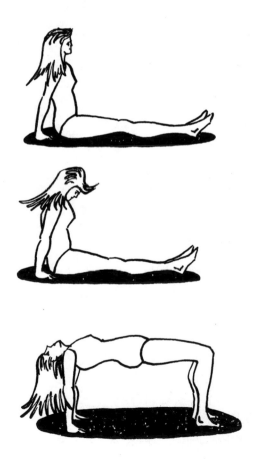

FIFTH RITE

Support yourself just off the floor, on straight arms and toes, hands and feet about two feet apart. Now lean your head back as far as you can, then inhaling deeply, raise your body as high as possible into an inverted V, bringing head forward to touch chin to chest. Tense all muscles through your body briefly, then, exhaling, return to starting position and again tense all muscles briefly, then relax and repeat.

~SIXTH RITE~

Begin in standing position. Bend over, bracing hands on knees, and force as much air as you can out of your lungs. Then straighten up, put hands on hips and push down, which raises the shoulders. Pull in your stomach as much as possible, holding your breath as long as you can, then exhale, relax, take several deep breaths and repeat. After 3 or 4 repetitions, you will feel that no more energy is available to raise up to the head and throughout the body, so of course there's no point in doing any more repetitions. Colonel Bradford recommended to do this when one felt a strong sexual urge, signaling a super-abundance of energy in the body, seeking release. As the earlier comments from Kyle Griffith showed, this Sixth Rite appears to be one variation of a number of techniques making up a whole science of Tantric "sex magic."

9 FREEING FROZEN EMOTIONAL ENERGY

T HIS BOOK IS CONCERNED with the liberation of the human spirit. The spirit is energy. Liberation of the spirit is not just a high-sounding ideal but can involve dramatic releases of blocked or dammed-up energy which vastly enhances one's vitality and joy of living.

Restriction or imprisonment of the spirit can have many forms. One can be physically tied up, imprisoned or handicapped. Such things can prevent a person from realizing his or her fullest creative potential, though history is full of examples of people who have accomplished outstanding things in spite of such physical restraints.

More subtle, and often more debilitating, are the internal restraints on the spirit; not obviously visible but nevertheless held within the mind and body and restricting the spirit's freedom at every moment, never allowing one to enjoy a single instant of complete joy in life.

Mental prejudice is one such internal restraint. The mind likes to run in the groove it is accustomed to; in the ruts it has worn deep. To be free sometimes requires an effort to pull the mind out of its habitual rut and set it to exploring new territory. The most common form of mental bondage is the confusion of information with knowledge. Your knowledge is what you know is true from your own experience. Information is hearsay that you have picked up and don't know if it is true or not. The fool will say, "If you don't accept Jesus you'll go to hell forever." The wise person might say, "I know a preacher who says that if you don't accept Jesus you'll go to hell forever." A fool will say, "I know that light travels 186,000 miles a second." A wise person might say, "My high school science book says that light travels 186,000 miles per second." A free person will not confuse his information with his knowledge.

And in the preceding chapters we have dealt with another important internal restriction on the spirit, that of toxemia and poisoning from unnatural food, which impairs the full functioning of the body and beclouds some of the important intuitive areas of the mind.

And now in this chapter I want to take up a third sort of internal restraint on the spirit, and that is the blockage of emotional energy. It is a fairly common problem that causes much misery for some people; though of course it is not virtually universal like cooked-food poisoning.

My understanding is that the great 20th-century pioneer in recognizing, describing, understanding the causes of and developing effective therapies for alleviating this sort of problem was Dr. Wilhelm Reich. Reich began studying psychology as a student of Freud. Freud had the insight that psychological problems or neuroses always involved impairment of free and healthy sexual functioning, but apparently never did really bring this insight down to earth and connect it with physical reality in a way that allowed him to really help people who suffered from such problems. Consequently, many people go through years and decades of Freudian-type psychoanalysis and don't make a dent in their problems.

Reich saw that psychological problems, or neuroses, always involved an actual physical constriction, blockage and restraint of emotional energies because of a chronic tension throughout the muscles of the body. The emotions and the sex drive involve the same energy, the same life-force. In all healthy people, surplus energy tends to accumulate, which creates a tension which seeks release in the orgasm, similar to the way the air under high pressure in a blown-up balloon seeks release. Reich saw that the person who "has problems," is neurotic, is unable to fully experience the orgasm or to express fully any strong emotion, whether it be joy, love, anger or grief. Such a person goes about in a state of continual frustration, seeing others freely expressing their joy and their anger, their love and their hate, but making a pathetic and grotesque parody and caricature of it when trying to express his or her own feelings. Normal people look at such a person and say, "What a nerd! Why doesn't he-or-she relax and act normal?" And the more kindly of them will give the person with such problems well-meaning advice like, "Just relax and quit worrying and just be yourself!" which is of course what the neurotic sufferer from such problems desperately wants to do more than anything else in the Six Universes but is utterly unable to do because of the chronic muscular tension, or "armoring" as Reich called it, which prevents the life-force, the emotional energy, from moving freely through the body.

The problem of emotional energy blockages generally originates in oppressive attitudes of parents toward their children. You often see parents attempting to shame and scold and bully their kids into a mold, into becoming what the parents think the child should be, instead of respecting what the kids naturally are and trying to help them develop along the lines of their natural potentials and inclinations. After 25 or 30 or more years of a health-destroying lifestyle with junk food, smoking and drinking and carrying the weight of the guilt complexes and fears that their parents gave them, many parents are pretty depleted of vitality themselves and they feel threatened and irritated by the innocent and exuberant vitality of their young children. And so, with sheer strength and clever mental sophistry on their side, the parents set out to break the spirit of their kids, to beat down their vitality and load them down with as much fear and guilt as these parents themselves are burdened with. It's a crime worse than murder that goes on virtually unnoticed, day after day and year after year in millions of homes around the world!

When a person does have this problem of armoring, life is a continual hell of frustration and disappointment that never lets up for a single instant. Every action, every word, has to be spoken and performed through a thick fog of pain and fear and anger, like trying to run under water. Somewhere deep down inside, one may feel full of fiery enthusiasm, with love and great ideas, may dream of shouting and singing and making grand, moving, inspiring speeches—but when the armored person tries to carry out such desires—all that comes out is a confused, stuttering, halting croak that everybody ignores and despises and laughs at.

Most people who have this problem of course aren't aware that they have a problem. They think that the continual inner torment of pain and guilt and fear that they feel is natural and healthy and normal and that people without such problems are acting perverse and evil and barbaric and especially the armored person feels that everybody is deliberately trying to hurt him (or her); when of course in fact they usually have no such intention at all but are just having fun.

The good news is that if a person does have this problem and recognizes it and wants to do something about it, there are ways to slowly and gradually release the blocked emotional energies, over a period of many years, involving a tremendous amount of hard and painful inner work on yourself. One might wonder, why do some people have to suffer so much with this sort of problem while others are completely free to have fun and enjoy life all their lives? The reason is that there is no fairness or justice or mercy in this world whatsoever.

I once had a friend who said that as a little girl, she saw all sorts of things happening that she didn't think were right. So she would always go around saying, "That's not fair! That's not fair!" And then one day somebody told her, "Who ever told you it was going to be fair?" And that's how it is in this world. There is no fairness or justice at all. Some people are very happy while others are perfectly miserable. Some are loaded with more wealth than they know what to do with while others must starve. And the only way out of it is if the suffering and starving people work very, very hard to improve their situation, and even then they may not succeed. Otherwise, it is very, very rare that the wealthy and happy people will do anything to help the less fortunate and often there's not much they can do even if they want to. And there certainly isn't any God or Christ or mystical Brotherhood that's going to help make things happier in this world over night.

As I said, this problem of emotional energy blockages or armoring is not universal, though the Reichian literature makes it sound like almost everybody suffers from it. I don't think so though. By my observation, I'd say that the significant majority of people don't have this problem. It is a common problem though, and worth writing about in this book because this is a book about healing and liberation of the spirit and I want to tell all I know that might help somebody. Even if it only helps one person it is still worthwhile. I get a channeled newsletter that asks readers to always ask themselves, "How many have you served, and how well?" Serving one is better than serving none.

I've had this problem of armoring very bad. Probably about as bad a case of it as anyone has ever had. I've been working very hard on solving it for a little over ten years now, and have made tremendous progress, though at the time of this writing I can feel I'm not quite free of it yet. Still have some more work to do.

So I'll tell you what I've done that has worked, and maybe somebody else will find something that has helped me, helpful to them also.

The first thing I found helpful in releasing myself from armoring, was Rebirthing. Rebirthing is a breathing technique, discovered or re-discovered by Leonard Orr and his associates in the early 1970's. I say re-discovered because Orson Bean in his book Me and The Orgone describes a breathing technique that he did as part of his Reichian Therapy, that is the same as Rebirthing. So apparently Reich discovered it some years before Leonard Orr. At any rate, I learned how to do Rebirthing from the book Rebirthing in the New Age by Leonard Orr and Sondra Ray. To do Rebirthing, you lie down comfortably in a place where you will not be disturbed for the next three hours. You then begin breathing deeply and rapidly, at least 40 breaths per minute, through the mouth, because you can't breathe deeply and rapidly enough through your nose. Another name for Rebirthing is Hyperventilation. Keep your breath continally moving so that you are not holding it up at any point. Typically after about 10 minutes of this, you begin to feel a tingling in your hands. The tingling grows stronger and spreads to your feet and often your chest, neck, and other parts of your body. You just keep on doing the breathing. Then, frequently, the hands and feet become cramped up and paralyzed. The experience may become very painful. Several times in Rebirthing sessions I felt such intense physical and emotional pain develop that I swore that if I lived through that session I would never do Rebirthing again. But whatever happens, however your hands become paralyzed, however much pain develops, you want to just keep on doing your deep, rapid breathing. If you stop while paralyzed you'll stay paralyzed until you take up the breathing again and finish your interrupted Rebirthing session.

So as you keep breathing, the pain, paralysis and tingling will gradually begin to weaken and disappear, to be replaced by a great sense of lightness and joy and release and relaxation. You'll feel that a weight has been taken off your shoulders and you feel lighter and happier about being alive. In Leonard Orr's terms, you will have discharged some "negative mental mass." In Reichian terms, you will have discharged some DOR, deadly orgone or stagnant life-force. Your Rebirthing session is over when the tingling has disappeared.

From this description, it might sound like Rebirthing is dangerous. But, as Leonard Orr says, "Rebirthing is safer than the public schools." To the best of my knowledge, of the tens of thousands and perhaps hundreds of thousand or even millions of people who have now done Rebirthing, nobody has ever been killed or permanently injured by it. Rebirthing is certainly safer than riding in a car or airplane or motorcycle, safer than taking a vaccination or undergoing surgery; all things that many people have died or become crippled from.

Some people involved in Rebirthing say that you should always be supervised by an experienced, well-trained Rebirther when you do your session. I suspect one of their motives in saying this is to drum up business because some people make a career of being Rebirthers and charge hefty fees of $40 and more to supervise a session. I did Rebirthing the first few times on my own and got excellent results. Then I hired a couple of professional Rebirthers to supervise me at 40 bucks a crack and got excellent results, though no better than when I was on my own. Then I did it again on my own and did just as well as when supervised by the pros. So I decided then I could do just as well on my own and not throw my money away on professional Rebirthers who often had an inflated opinion of their own value. I have noticed though that many people are rather lazy and timid about doing things like Rebirthing on their own without "expert supervision." Such people will of course want and need to hire Rebirthers to do this process.

The reason it is called Rebirthing is because Leonard Orr was originally seeking a way to relive his birth, remember it so fully that all the pain and trauma involved in it would be released from his body, leaving him free to enjoy life fully. He began experimenting, immersing himself in a hot tub and breathing deeply through a snorkel. It worked. He recalled his birth and released negative mental mass from his system. Later he found that the breathing was the important thing and the hot tub really wasn't necessary.

Rebirthing is a good process, but conceptually and philosophically I found the Rebirthing movement to lack a clear goal, a definite aim that you were trying to achieve by doing Rebirthing. Rebirthers talked rather vaguely about achieving a "Breath Release" but never did quite make it clear what a Breath Release was. Actually every successful Rebirthing session produces some degree of breath release, since chronic tension and constriction of the diaphragm and other muscles used in breathing, are involved in every case of armoring. But there is no one big sudden earth-shaking Breath Release that puts the practitioner of Rebirthing into Endless Bliss; rather each session of Rebirthing produces a measure of breath release, of release of tension from the diaphragm and other breathing muscles, and the cumulative result of many Rebirthing sessions can add up to considerably more freedom in breathing.

By way of contrast, Reich in his therapy set a clear and attainable goal of re-establishment of orgastic potency; that is, the ability to fully experience the orgasm throughout the whole bodt, which requires that all the muscles be able to relax fully.

I did Rebirthing for about a year and got a lot of benefit from it. Then I was introduced to—

Kundalini Maha Yoga. This is a system for raising the Kundalini, or Orgone, or Sex Energy, up from the base of the spine to the top of the head. Along the way, the stimulated movement and flowing of this energy gradually "purifies" the nervous system—dissolves energy blockages that may be held within it. The primary purpose of Kundalini Maha Yoga is to stimulate activity of the higher chakras—those concerned with matters beyond one's immediate personal desires for comfort, wealth and power. In the majority of people, only the lower chakras appear to be active and influencing their thought and behavior. These are concerned with sexual desire and with the desire to accumulate comfort, wealth, prestige and influence. With the higher chakras activated, one becomes more exploratory in consciousness, more pioneering, interested in growth and unfoldment, in looking at new possibilities, in art and science for their own sake rather than just for immediate commercial application. For instance, before I had done any of this Yoga, I was primarily concerned with commercial application of art, in how I could immediately use whatever skills in sign painting and drawing that I had, to make money. After doing Kundalini Maha Yoga for a while, I began to be more interested in Fine Art, in Art as an expressive and exploratory activity for its own sake, as a means of gaining insight into nature's creative principles by experiencing them at work through my own mind and body. This I now see as the primary value of art. It is a means of understanding Nature's creative principles from the inside, from observing them at work in yourself. The same life-force that motivates a painter also makes a tree grow. The principles that make a beautiful picture are the same as the principles which make a successful universe. In our creative work we create life-forms and worlds and universes. You don't have to wait for any hot-shot scientist to create life in a test tube. You create a living organism when you write a poem, paint a picture, build a table or whatever.

With practice of Kundalini Maha Yoga I found my interests expanding in all sorts of directions. I became interested in New-Age science, flying saucers and fuelless power generators and so forth. I became interested in economics and politics, especially in how these systems can be made to work justly, for the benefit of all. Unfortunately, as mentioned, most people appear to have their consciousness all in the lower chakras so they are not interested in how to make the economic system work to everyone's greatest benefit. They are only interested in grabbing as much of the pie for themselves as they can. As the American economy gets worse and worse, most people do not ask, "How can we fix this thing up and make it work well for everyone?" Instead they ask, "How can I screw my neighbor and grab some of his share of the pie for myself?" Unfortunately most people apparently do not see that the surest way to ensure continuing prosperity for yourself is to get it working so that all your neighbors can be prosperous too. As some famous senator pointed out, it's difficult to sell something to a man with no money.

The way Kundalini Maha Yoga worked is, first you had to get a Shaktipat initiation from a Guru capable of giving this. Shaktipat means transference of energy. The transference of the Guru's energy to you is for the purpose of awakening and activating your Kundalini. Then you practice meditation by concentrating either in your forehead at the third eye spot or at the top of your head. I had better luck with the top of the head. This concentration by the principle of "energy follows thought," draws the Kundalini energy into the higher chakras. As it moves up the spine, it tends to gradually loosen and dissolve any energy blockages that hinder its flow.

I have lost touch with the Guru who gave me my Shaktipat initiation so I'm sorry but I can't tell you where to go to get one yourself. His name was Dhyanyogi Madhusudandas and I believe his organization is still active somewhere in the U.S., under the name of Dhyanyoga Center. So if you hear of it you'll know where to go. I have not practiced Kundalini Maha Yoga much in the last few years because I found some other things which I felt helped me more. The first of these was—

Re-evaluation Counseling, or RC. This is a system for "Discharging emotional distress," which is the same thing as armor removal, DOR removal, and removal of negative mental mass. RC was developed by Harvey Jackins and his associates, beginning in the early 1950s in Seattle, Washington, and has since gained many thousands of practitioners worldwide, though the RC organizations tend to maintain a low profile and do not seek publicity, because of their well-founded belief that oppressive, authoritarian societies such as the one we live in, will always do their best to crush, destroy and stamp out any visible mass-movements which seek to make people more free and happy and have practical and effective means by which to do so. So maybe RC won't like the publicity I'm giving them here now, but I'm going to do it because describing a few basic, simple RC techniques might help somebody out there somewhere.

RC, or Co-counseling as it is also often called, usually involves two people who take turns counselling each other. The Counsellee may talk about any of a great number of possible topics. She or he may talk about the day just past and incidents in it, the week just past, the distant past, her or his feelings on various social issues—and the object of the Counsellor is to encourage, and create a safe space, for the Counsellee to express any and all strong feelings and strong emotions aroused by the discussion, which in other circumstances she or he would tend to feel uncomfortable or shy about expressing. This expression of strong and sincere emotion in the presence of the Counselor tends to relieve chronic tension and increase the Counsellee's vitality and rationality. Often the use of RC techniques will bring about contact with and discharge of long-repressed emotions. One may break into spontaneous fits of laughter, or anger, or grief. These are signs of really productive discharge of long-suppressed emotional distress.

I'll describe now a very simple and basic RC technique which readers may, if they wish, begin using immediately to get a taste of these methods and their effects. It is called, "praising yourself." The two co-counselling partners sit facing each other and looking into each other's eyes. Okay, let's say you are the Counsellee. You think of what is your worst problem, the worst inadequacy you have, the thing that causes you the most grief and misery in life. For example, suppose that you think you are a coward, scared of your own shadow. You run for your life whenever a turtle comes charging down the road. Okay; now you turn it around and make a positive statement in affirmation of the virtue that you think you lack. For instance, look your partner squarely in the eye and say, "I am the bravest and boldest son of a bitch to ever walk the face of this Earth! Paul Bunyan watch out, I'm gonna whip your ass!" Say it with all the force and firmness and sincerity at your command. Say it loud. Say it like you are a high-priced lawyer defending a food-company executive who puts moldy peaches laced with illegal insecticides into his baby-food jars, and you're trying to convince the jury that the guy is a saint.

If you do it right, and really say it loud and firm and sincere and not just in a shy little pipsqueak, what will probably happen is that you will burst out laughing uncontrollably. That is very good. That is the discharge you are trying to get, the expression of suppressed emotion and release of long-standing chronic tension. Okay, after you've stopped laughing, pull yourself together and look your partner in the eye and do it again. After a half hour or so you switch roles. And after a half hour of discharge like this you'll probably find yourself feeling noticeably lighter, freer, more joyful and intrinsically happy about being alive, like a weight has been taken off your shoulders. If you want further information about RC and Co-counseling, I suggest read *The Benign Reality* and other books by Harvey Jackins and other RC authors. They also publish some magazines. The publisher is Rational Island Publishers of Seattle, Washington.

I found RC to have the same drawback or failing as Rebirthing, and that was the lack of a clear goal and end to be attained by all this therapeutic work. The RC People I knew said that nobody had ever succeeded in discharging all their distress. They seemed to see RC work as an ongoing lifelong thing, that you could thus become gradually more and more free of such distress but never totally free of it. Somehow I didn't want to buy that idea. And that led me to become very interested when I heard about—

Reichian psychology. I was introduced to this subject by the writings of Michael Tobin of Ireland. From about 1979 to 1987, he and Caroline Kuijper prolifically wrote and published a series of tremendously powerful and inspiring bulletins on the problems of the world and their visions and activities for solving them. It is some of the very best new-age writing thus far produced and someday I hope some smart new-age publisher will see the tremendous opportunity available and collect all these bulletins together and re-publish them as a book. Someday soon.

At any rate, one of the major items that Tobin and Kuijper were promoting was Reichian psychology. To summarize, once more—Dr. Wilhelm Reich began as a psychology student under Freud. Freud had the insight that psychological problems or neuroses originated in a disturbance of natural sexual functioning, but he never did develop this insight into an effective therapy for such problems. Reich saw that such psychological problems or neuroses always involved constricted breathing and chronic tension throughout the muscular system of the body, which prevented his patients from expressing strong emotion fully and freely and from experiencing the orgasm fully. He proceeded to develop methods of working on the muscles and on the breathing so as to release this chronic tension or armoring and restore emotional freedom to his patients. He saw this work as having vast sociological and political implications. He saw authoritarian and oppressive political structures as rooted in the sexual repression of the average individual. A sexually repressed individual lacks self-confidence and inner direction and therefore is easily led around by leaders and authorities and dictators. Therefore oppressive and authoritarian rulers always make it their first item of business to prevent people from enjoying a free, natural, healthy and satisfying sex life. They try to make everyone think in terms of what is right and wrong and what is your duty rather than in terms of what do you really want and what really makes you happiest. They try to impose morality rather than liberate everyone's natural love and goodness.

I could see I had this problem of armoring pretty bad and Michael Tobin's writing made me want to try the Reichian therapy to solve it. So I investigated the possibility of working with a Reichian therapist. I soon found out that Reichian therapists charge an arm and a leg and ten pounds of flesh and a poor working person like myself couldn't afford them. So I said to myself, to hell with the professionals, I'll figure out how to do this myself—in the grand old American handyman do-it-yourself tradition.

I could afford a few books, so I read everything on Reichian therapy that I could get my hands on. I read Orson Bean's *Me and the Orgone*, Reich's *The Function of the Orgasm*, Dr. Elsworth Baker's *Man in the Trap* and some writings by Dr. Charles Kelly. These gave me enough hints to get started.

The first technique I worked with and found helpful goes like this: You kneel on the floor with a big pillow in front of you. Now you start breathing deeply and rhythmically, through the nose, but you don't have to breathe as rapidly as in Rebirthing. Now you start rhythmically pounding on the pillow with your fists also, and relax inside as you do this and allow any spontaneous expression of suppressed energies which are contacted by this method, to proceed. For instance if you suddenly feel real mad and want to pound the devil out of the pillow, you go ahead and do it. It's similar to the discharge in RC work. It will probably take 2 or 3 sessions working with this technique to relax enough inside to let it work. At first when you do this technique you tend to feel embarrassed, like you are making a real horse's ass out of yourself. After 2 or 3 sessions like this, though, you become able to relax and let it work.

After working with this technique a while, I became more and more aware of my breathing and its relation to the tensions in my body, so that at any time I was able to relax and breathe in such a way as not to suppress the discharge of these tensions but to allow it to proceed in a natural way. And this is the technique I now use. You could maybe call it "relaxed and surrendered breathing," and it's very simple and natural, but I can't really describe it in writing. Well, I can, sort of. The armored person's body is always trying to express and discharge the suppressed energies, but the breathing pattern such a person has developed prevents it. It just takes a little relaxation at key points in the breathing pattern—either the end of the exhalation or the beginning of the inhalation—to allow the body's natural efforts to express withheld, suppressed energies, to proceed.

Another technique I have worked with some is what Reich called "Releasing the gag reflex." To do this, you stick 2 or 3 fingers down your throat as far as you can and try to make yourself vomit. Take a deep breath and do it again. And again. Very effective for working on diaphragm armoring. The best time to do it is early morning before you have had breakfast, for obvious reasons.

Another technique which can be helpful in working off armoring is Bhagwan Shree Rajneesh's Dynamic Meditation, described in his book *Meditation, The Art of Ecstasy*. The meditation has five segments; it is the first two that concern us for our present purposes. Each segment is to last 10 minutes. During the first ten minutes, standing up, you breathe as deeply and rapidly as you possibly can, through the nose. During the second ten minutes you "let out your madness," that is, allow the expression and discharge of any suppressed emotional energies that may have been stirred up by the breathing in the first ten minutes. You may feel like shouting, crying, stomping around, whatever. Do it. Again, it generally takes working with this technique 2 or 3 or 4 times before you get relaxed enough about it and quit worrying about what a fool you are making of yourself, to make it work.

There are several other therapeutic systems that I am slightly acquainted with but have not worked with myself, that have similar goals and puposes to those mentioned above. For instance, there is Rolfing, which works to correct poor posture by discharging suppressed emotions which can create poorly balanced posture. And there is Primal Therapy, which evidently is very similar to Reichian Therapy. In fact, Dr. Charles Kelly, a neo-

Reichian practitioner from California, in a publication of his that I read, said that Dr. Arthur Janov, the creator of Primal Therapy, actually studied with Reich, but does not mention this in his books on Primal Therapy. Maybe he feared his professional reputation would suffer if he acknowledged association with a man that the Science Establishment still considers a crackpot.

So, as I said at the beginning, this problem of armoring or suppressed emotional energy does not appear to me to be universal or nearly so, but it nevertheless is a common problem which causes a great deal of unnecessary misery for quite a few people. So I hope this chapter may serve to help some of those people overcome this problem.

And so, dear Readers, this concludes my little book. As I said, I hope it helps somebody somewhere sometime and plants a few little seeds here and there that will eventually grow to help create a New Age of health, happiness, freedom, justice, true creativity and true progress.

The aim of this book is to help people find the True Center, from which proceeds life-force and freedom and creativity. That center is the Earth, the Great Mind of Mother Earth. Nature follows this Center and people are supposed to also. But people pollute and poison their consciousness with DOR, dark energy, stagnant energy, anti-life force, and this DOR-smog covers up their inner eyes so they can't see clearly what's really good for them and what's not. It hides the light of the True Center and so they follow False Centers instead: Governments, Universities, Religions, Theories and Philosophies and their own egos. And I think the most important, most significant source, the one that has caused the most harm to humanity's course of evolution, the worst source of this DOR—pollution of consciousness in virtually every person on the face of the Earth—is from cooked-food eating. And I expect the only people who will disagree with me will be ones who haven't made the experiments I have made—to live on all raw food for at least a year.

My publisher has told me that probably many sick people will read this book, looking for help, and it would be a good idea to gear my writing towards trying to help such people. Well, I hope I have helped readers to understand that the cause of most diseases, probably about 90% of them or maybe even more— is the poisoning of the body by toxemia, the wastes and excess mucus accumulated by eating too much unnatural food, junk food, which your body cannot digest and dispose of the wastes properly and efficiently. Thus the diseases which have this cause can be overcome by cleaning out the body and living on natural foods, which the body can digest and eliminate efficiently.

In addition to this, some foods are reported as having special strengthening and healing values, especially the chlorophyll-rich foods like wheat grass and blue-green algae. I have not personally experienced or witnessed such strengthening and healing qualities in these foods, but people who sound trustworthy to me have reported these things. So they're sure worth a try. Blue-green algae and Barley Green you have to buy somewhere. Ask around at the nearest health food store. You can grow wheatgrass yourself. Get wheat seeds that haven't been treated with some sort of fungicide or herbicide or insecticide or rodenticide; soak them overnight in water, plant them in a tray with about an inch of soil, or in the ground, plant them thickly so that it's like a carpet of wheat seeds, close together, even touching, and then keep them adequately watered. Then when they get about 6 inches high you mow them off near the base but don't pull up the roots. Chew up the wheat grass and swallow the juice and spit out the pulp, or put the wheatgrass in a salad, or put it through a special Grass Juicer (don't foul up your Champion trying to juice wheatgrass in it) and squeeze out a little glass of juice and drink it real fresh. See Viktoras Kulvinskas's and Ann Wigmore's books for the inside dope on wheatgrass, how to grow it and eat it. They're the pros on this subject; I'm just an amateur.

One more book I want to highly recommend to any readers that think I've got any of my marbles straight—it's called Star Signs by Linda Goodman. Terrific. First book I've read that's got me convinced physical immortality is really possible. Others I've read on the subject, like Leonard Orr and Sondra Ray—well, it sounded like it was a neat idea they were having fun kicking around, but Linda Goodman sounds like she bloody well KNOWS it's for real. So I can highly recommend her book to any of my readers who think my opinion is worth at least as much as a wooden nickel.

Actually, I'm really writing in hopes of getting people who are not really sick to try raw food. If I can help sick people, great, but I'd especially like for young and healthy people to take up raw food diet so they could become even healthier and use their new energy and new insight for a very productive lifetime of high-level creative work which would really help lots of people and help straighten up the damn mess on this potentially Paradise Planet. Unfortunately people tend to be smug and complacent. If they're doing pretty good, they're not interested in growth. They just want to maintain thier comfortableness, if they don't have really bad problems and are pretty comfortable. It's usually only the people who have really serious problems that look for improvement. They start off looking for healing and find that healing leads to growth and then want to keep on growing.

Anyway, the value of raw food diet is not that it gives you a mystical experience of unity with Nature like a drug trip, or even that it makes your personal sex life a lot more fun and satisfying. It does, of course. As Dick Gregory said in his book, nothing beats clean sex. But the main value of raw food diet is that it can give you so much more energy and insight with which to do creative work for everybody's benefit. So it's best if people take it up when they're still young and healthy. But I certainly don't want to discourage anybody, any condition, any age from taking it up.

There's an old saying, "Better to light a candle than curse the darkness." It's a nice sentiment, but who is such a perfect Pollyanna that all they do is light candles and never curse the darkness? Nobody that I know; the people I know that light the brightest candles also do the loudest cursing. So I want to change the saying to, "Light a candle while you curse the darkness." This book has been one of my attempts to do so. I hope you've had fun reading it, and that you're a healthier, happier person the rest of your natural life.

APPENDIX A

The Influence of Heat Labile Factors on Nutrition in Oral Development and Health

By F.M. Pottenger, Jr., M.D.
D.G. Simonsen, Ph.D.

From the *Research Department, Pottenger Sanatorium, Monrovia, California*, Read at the *42nd Annual Convention, Southern Calif. State Dental Association.*

SEVEN YEARS AGO, when we started to totally adrenalectomize cats for the purpose of standardizing cortical extracts, we had a large supply of cooked meats left over from the table, so we used them as the total meat supply for our animals. Our operative morality was high, and in trying to find the reason for this, we noted that the cats showed certain deficiencies. We found that all of the animals showed a decrease in reproductive efficiency and that the kittens showed certain deformities and malfunctions. Inasmuch as these animals were given market grade raw milk and cod liver oil, along with the portions of liver, tripe, sweetbreads, brains, heart and muscle, we were at a loss to explain the reason, for it had been taught that such a diet contained the necessary substances to maintain animals in a condition of health.

However, when the food demand of our cats exceeded the supply of cooked scraps and it became necessary to purchase extra meat, we fed it as raw food. We at first fed the raw scraps to cats in one particular pen. The change in the animals in that pen compared with the others was almost unbelievable, and demanded explanation; so the present study was undertaken.

The first observation was made purely by chance, but in attempting to ascertain the cause, we have tried to control the conditions of the experiments in every possible way. In this paper, we shall report only those observations which have a definite bearing on the oral development and health of these animals. No attempt will be made to correlate the other changes in the animals studied with malformations found in the human. However, the similarity is so obvious that parallel pictures will suggest themselves.

FEEDING THE ANIMALS. We have found that cats from healthy parents, if maintained on our optimum diet all their lives, will show normal development, and be able to reproduce their kind, generation after generation, without evidence of deterioration.

This diet consists of raw meat, including viscera, bones, a small amount of raw milk, and cod liver oil.

The deficient diet which we use consists of meat prepared for human consumption, muscle as well as such viscera as liver, heart, brains, kidneys, sweetbreads, cooked by boiling, baking, roasting, frying and broiling. This is supplemented by milk and cod liver oil, the same as given in the raw meat diet.

The fact that the meat is cooked is sufficient to cause the adult cat and its offspring to show the degenerations such as we shall later describe.

CLASSIFICATION OF TERMS. *Nutrition* is the sum total of metabolic processes which maintain the tissues of the individual in a state of health or disease, in contradistinction to *diet*, which is the food intake of the individual.

First generation deficient animals consist of animals which have had the opportunity to reach maturity under optimum conditions and upon which deficiency is then imposed. They have, therefore, reached maturity without interference in their normal physiology.

Second generation deficient animals are the offspring of female cats of the first generation upon which the deficient diet has been imposed for varying periods of time, but including the entire gestation and nursing period.

Third generation deficient animals are those kittens born to second generation deficient cats which have been maintained on the deficient diets all ther lives. So far, we have not been able to produce kittens beyond the third generation, when the ancestors have been continuously fed on heat processed foods.

REGENERATING CATS. If a cat of the first generation is placed and continued on the optimum diet after giving birth to a deficient litter, these kittens are classified as regenerating kittens of the first order.

Kittens born to second generation cats which are placed on optimum diets are classified as regenerating kittens of the second order. So far there have been no regenerating kittens of the third order.

In the production of deficient kittens, the degenerating processes are progressive. Certain of the deficiencies may or may not show in the first generation. If present, these are accentuated in the second, and even more accentuated in the third generation. In our attempts to regenerate kittens on optimum diets, it seems as though these deformities become less and less in intensity from one generation to the next. It appears from our present study that optimum diets for four generations will be required to bring back cats of the second generation deficiency to anything like their normal efficiency.

According to our experience, once a female cat has been subjected to the deficient diet for a period of twelve to eighteen months or more, her reproductive efficiency is so reduced that she will never again give birth to normally developed kittens. Even after three or four years, her kittens still show facial and dental imperfections.

As far as possible, the same male cat is used each year for breeding. He is selected as the best of our animals from the standpoint of development and physical fitness. So we are studying the deficiency as imposed on the offspring by the chemistry of the female alone. We have bred a few cats where both parents are deficient. It is too early to make a definite statement, but it is suggestive that deficiency of paternity may affect the offspring as well as deficiency of maternity.

TISSUE CHANGES ABOUT THE TEETH. We have yet to see degenerative changes in the soft tissues of the cats of healthy parentage maintained on the optimum diet. Salivary calculi do not develop. Some of the small, central teeth may be lost in fighting, and other traumatic injuries may occur; but we have never seen evidence of infection in these healthy animals.

The deficient animals differ greatly in this respect. The first generation of cooked meat animals may exhibit merely a simple gingivitis, but usually incrustations of salivary calculi appear, and continue to increase, whether the cat is maintained on a deficient diet or returned to optimum diet. As these salivary deposits increase, the gums become spongy, and this is usually followed by infection, with the presence of pus. Resorption of the alveolar processes and in extreme cases, osteomyelitis takes place. Abscesses perforating the cheek have been noted, and loss of teeth is quite common.

In spite of these findings, we have not seen evidences of dental caries in the teeth of these deficient animals.

If the cat is on a deficient diet, returning the animal to optimum diet is not sufficient to arrest the degenerative changes noted above. The animal has lost something through the use of deficient foods which is necessary to its nutrition and general dental health. It has lost its ability to resist dental diseases and prevent formation of salivary calculi. In three to five years, nearly all of the incisors, most of the molars and premolars are lost. The canines seem to be slightly more resistant. When a female cat, after being carried on a deficient diet, is returned to the optimum diet and continued on it, she reproduces better kittens each year, for a period of time.

The second generation deficient cats exhibit conditions that are similar to those found in the first generation deficient cats. However, a mild gingivitis is frequently seen in the young kittens, and bleeding and spongy gums before the eruption of the primary teeth is common. While the canines seem to be the best protected of all the teeth of the first generation cat, in the second generation deficient cat, active root resorption with osteoporotic areas at the apex of the teeth frequently causes the loss of these teeth, before the posterior teeth are lost. Quite frequently the conical apex of the perfect canine becomes squared off and irregular as root resorption occurs. Loosening of the canines in their sockets frequently causes animals great discomfort.

The third generation of deficient kittens does not live long enough to show the development of all the conditions noted above. They do, however, show an extreme gingivitis and tenderness of their gums in early life, even to a much greater degree than is seen in the second generation of kittens.

REGENERATING KITTENS. In spite of the fact that these cats have come from mothers on optimum diets, and they themselves have been on such all their lives, it is interesting to note that often these animals suffer from as severe and crippling a gingivitis, salivary calculi, resorption of the alveolar processes, pyorrhea, and loss of teeth as do the animals of the first and second generations on deficient diets. In this case, something has occurred to the physiological efficiency or nutrition of these animals before they were born, or during their nursing period that has not allowed them to develop a proper protective mechanism.

CHANGES IN DENTAL CONFIGURATION. The X-ray of the skull of fully developed adult shows poor occlusion. The development of the whole face is materially interfered with.

The skull of the second generation deficient adult is smaller than that of the first generation of the same age. The skull of the third generation is materially smaller than that of the second generation.

Differential growths are frequently seen. In some instances the anterior movement of the face through the central portion is apparently retarded more than the anterior movement of the jaw. Failure in the lateral movement of the face causes material narrowing of the mandible and maxillary portion, so that frequently there is insufficient room for a complete set of six central incisors to descend into place.

Some of these teeth fail to come into place at all because of narrowing and foreshortening of the dental arches. Likewise, the canine teeth, instead of making a graceful arch covered completely by the lips, frequently protrude laterally, so that it is difficult for the animal to properly close his mouth, and drooling ensues.

In some of the third generation deficient kittens, the failure of the anterior movement of the jaw has been so great that the posterior molars, instead of being embedded in the corpus of the mandible, remain in the ramus, and the crown of the tooth, instead of being parallel to the floor of the mouth, is definitely perpendicular to it.

These developmental changes of the face can be readily summarized as follows: (1) A lessening of the anterior-posterior and transverse diameters of the dental arch. (2) An apparent alteration of the angle of the corpus of the mandible to the ramus. (3) An apparent failure in the anterior development of the forward movement of the face. (4) A lessening in the development of the frontal sinuses. (5) An increase in the angle formed by the roof of the mouth and the base of the brain.

THE CALCIUM CONTENT OF BONES. To the dentist, the calcium content of the bone with which he is dealing is of great importance. We have examined the calcium content of the femurs of all cats coming to autopsy. In analyzing these femurs, we find that the total amount of calcium in the fresh bone is approximately twice that of the phosphorus. The normal adult cat shows a range from 12 to 17 percent calcium by weight. The calcium content of the femur of the normal second generation kitten up to one year of age falls between 8 and 12 percent. The deficient kitten of the second generation up to one year of age falls between 3½ and 7 percent of calcium. The third generation deficient cat may fall to the remarkable low of from 1½ to 3 percent calcium.

The bones of these third generation cats are soft, like sponge rubber. They show spontaneous fractures on the slightest provocation, which usually heal. They commonly show epiphyseal slips and injuries to the vertebrae. The bones of the mandible are just as soft as other bones. This is shown by the fact that the teeth can be easily moved by a slight touch of the fingers.

POROSITY OF BONES. Just as the calcium apparently diminishes from the first through the second and third generation, so is there a concomitant marked increase in the porosity of the bones. This we have studied particularly in X-rays of the zygomatic arch. Here we find that the trabecular structures seem to be fairly constant in mesh throughout life. In well developed cats, this trabecular structure is silk-like in fineness, but seems to vary slightly in width according to the amount of calcium in the bone.

The second generation deficient animals, however, show a coarser trabeculation, while third generation shows a very coarse framework. Trabeculation of the various generations might well be compared as follows: That of the first generation animal shows the fineness of a silk scarf; that of the second generation deficient animal, that of the plain cotton handkerchief; while that of the third generation is more like that of mosquito netting. Just as these three types of structures vary in fineness, so does their ability to support the teeth vary.

MECHANISM OF CHANGES. We are not in a position to state the exact nature of these changes. It is possible that dietary deficiency works partly through some of the endocrine organs. It may be that the pituitary, as described by Mortimer[1], is the organ to be suspected. On the other hand, we have been particularly impressed with the possibility that the thyroid may be an important secondary factor in the production of these facial deformities. It is well known to all endocrinologists that thyroid deficiency produces marked disturbance in osseous development. It is very interesting that we have been able to correlate certain of the facial types found in the kittens with thyroid deficiencies found in the female cats as they have come to autopsy. The facial configuration found in these kittens in which thyroid deficiencies are proven in the mothers are similar to what we would expect to find in the children of thyroid deficient women. Gonadal deficiencies may likewise play an important role in the deficient development of these animals.

Of the second generation male cats, 83 percent, on pathological examination, have been found to be functionally sterile, that is, they exhibit no spermatozoa. Fifty-three percent of the females show only primordial ova. However, the thyroid has been shown deficient in about 53 percent of both sexes. We likewise have found in these animals other evidences which are frequently associated in human pathology with thyroid deficiency, such as delay in the ossification of the carpal bones, closure of the epiphyses, slow dentition, and the lessened calcium content of the bones.

DISCUSSION. We are presenting our findings as we have noted them over a period of seven years. We do not know what factors are destroyed by heat processed foods. We do not believe that the deficiency is due to lack of Vitamin A because we have supplied about 4,000 I.U. a week in the cod liver oil. Since the cats are in open pens and are exposed to the sunlight, and in addition receive 500 I.U. of Vitamin D in their cod liver oil, there should be sufficient of this vitamin in their diet. Bills[2] states that certain sterols are present in the skin, in wool greases and in the preen gland of birds which may have a conditioning action on skin, hair and feathers. Since cats lick their fur, it is reasonable to assume that they receive some Vitamin D from this source. Elvehjem[3] and his colleagues have shown that meat contains approximately 3 I.U. of Vitamin B[1] per gram. Our cats consume from 70 to 100 grams of meat per day, thus receiving from 210 to 300 I.U. of Vitamin B[1] per day. Since the daily human requirement of B[1] is from 200 to 500 I.U. (according to Williams and Spies[4]) it would seem that these cats are receiving an adequate supply of Vitamin B[1]. The cats receive a small amount of Vitamin C in the milk which averages from 5 to 8 mg. of cevitamic acid per liter. Vitamin E, which occurs in small amounts in dairy products and meats, is relatively thermostable and should be present in both diets.

We are not prepared to discuss the rest of the vitamins at this time. On the other hand, in accounting for these deficiencies, we wish to call attention to the fact that heat precipitates hydrophylic colloids, and therefore materially alters the state of the food, and similarly interferes with digestion and assimilation. Likewise, we have reason to believe that meat may be a source of necessary hormones which are as important as vitamins in the proper development of animals depending upon carnivorous diets. Certain hormones, such as the adrenal cortex and insulin and others are definitely thermolabile, and are destroyed at a moderate temperature, even that used in the pasteurization of milk. We know that hormones circulate in the tissues, and so it is not beyond reason that those portions of animals which are used for food may contain them in varying amounts.

That the destruction of these elements by heat may be a contributing factor in the production of the deficiency which we have noted is not a far fetched suggestion. We have noted experimentally that the adrenal cortical hormone is efficacious in aiding these second generation deficient cats to return to normal physiological reaction. We have particularly noted a material improvement in their reproductive efficiency.

While these findings might be considered somewhat pessimistic when they are translated into terms of human deficiency, yet there are certain redeeming factors to be taken into consideration.

On the other hand, in accounting for their deficiencies, I wish to call attention to the fact that these animals were in pens, and were so controlled that the only food that they obtained was that which we gave them. Man is rarely restricted in his dietary to a totally cooked food ration. It must be remembered that these cats do receive raw milk of market grade, and that this is not sufficient to overcome the effects of cooked meat. Man seems to be more like a rat, having greater vitality than the cat, and he can apparently respond to deficient conditions in a better manner. Nevertheless, the changes found in cats are comparable to many of those which we see in human beings. Moreover, we are being told today by the anthropologists that civilized man is physically steadily on the down grade. May not the heat processing to which we are subjecting a great portion of our foods be a factor in this downward trend? One of your colleagues, Dr. Weston A. Price[5], has most dramatically charted the degeneration of man. We have tried to show it to you as it may be produced in the cat. If it is true in human beings as in cats that the deficiency of the mother is impressed upon the third and fourth generations under optimum conditions of life, it is a serious challenge to modern civilization to seek out and correct the causes of these deficiencies.

Such changes can be brought about, but only if mankind is willing to change his habits of life. This is the problem of health-education. We have shown, in a limited clinical practice, that the human being can materially improve, but to do so requires hygienic living and a vital diet, both of which civilization spurns.

BIBLIOGRAPHY

1. Mortimer, II. Quoted in: Price, Weston A.: Nutrition and Physical Degeneration. Paul B. Hoeber, Inc., New York. P. 363, 1939.
2. Bills, Charles F. Physiological Reviews, Vol. 15, No. 1, 1935.
3. Michelsen, O., H.A. Waismann and C.A. Elvehjem. Journal of Nutrition, 17:269, 1939.
4. Williams, R.R. and T.D. Spies. Vitamin B-1 and Its Use in Medicine. The Macmillan Company, New York, P. 103, 1939.
5. Price, Weston A. Nutrition and Physical Degeneration. Paul Hoeber, Inc., New York, 1939.

APPENDIX B

COSMIC CRUSADE
by Michael Tobin

I MENTIONED THE WRITING of the Irishman Michael Tobin earlier in the chapter on releasing emotional energy blocks, and want to include here a sample of this writing. This one was written January 28th, 1984.

Our homeland planet is today in the iron grip of Technocratic Man, a most ferociously anti-life tyrant, whose very existence poses a death threat to the whole living earthly scheme. This monstrous devil incarnate is the final sick product of Patriarchal Society in its end time. He is an evil social cancer of the worst possible kind, whose life-killing poisons have infected the hearts, minds and the souls of millions of people the world over. And through deadening their most precious faculty of conscience, these unfortunate humans have unwittingly allowed themselves to become his willing slaves. The terrestrial situation is now so grave that nothing less than the total elimination of this fearsome technocratic psychic plague will save the living earth from the most terrible harm and allow its further development as a psycho-ecosystem.

Let no one doubt for a moment that Mother Nature, who has so carefully fostered terrestrial evolution for so long, is preparing a frightful end for technocracy. The writing is truly on the wall so far as the technocratic beast is concerned. It has taken nearly five billion years of earth time for the terrestrial system to evolve this far. Nature has spent most of this vast interval in weaving a web of life of the most intricate kind around our little planet. We ourselves, in fact, are in no way the top of an imaginary 'tree of evolution.' And we came into existence solely because the terrestrial web needed a nervous system to complete it. This is what the bio-social history of humankind has been about over the course of the last four million years or so. We were certainly not created just to have humans on our planet—to become arrogant parasites lording it over creation. The main reason we were produced by the terrestrial evolutionary thrust was to perform a vital function in the earth's bio-system. In this respect, we are on a par with earthworms and micro-organisms. Homo sapiens would do well to remember that he is merely one of many humanoid species which have been evolved by nature in the course of developing a properly functioning terrestrial nervous system, and that he is most surely not the last of these humanoid forms.

So far as the terrestrial web of life is concerned, an essential component of its nervous system is that the humans composing it should be creative forms with freedom of will. But such developed creatures can be of value to the forces of terrestrial evolution only if humanity at this point in time chooses to work with them—chooses to become the primary instrument through which the Divine Design for the web of life can be fully realized in practice. Unfortunately, the great creative potential embodied in the make-up of existing humankind has been taken over by technocratic man, whose mushrooming megalomania no longer knows any bounds. But, however great is the technological power of this emotionally, psychically, and spiritually crippled cretin, it is as nothing compared with the awesome might of mother nature—of Spirit who is the very cosmos itself. And a primary fact about our times is that mother nature is making ready to wipe the terrestrial slate clean—to start afresh with a new human species—a new humanity which can and will act in her best interests.

Now, traditional patriarchal man, because of his fragmented psyche, believed there was a split between matter and spirit. Neo-patriarchal technocratic man, by having a schizoid make-up, lives in his intellect while being totally alienated from nature, and is completely unable to find the divine in anything. But the fully integrated individual of the new humanity will experience the divine in everything. The whole cosmic scheme will appear as it actually is: an ever-developing spiritual process—the process of the materialization of spirit—the process of the evolution of spirit in material form. Yes, the new humanity, through having a natural emotional/psychic structure, together with an almost infinite potential for ethereal creative expression in material form, will intimately know spirit as the immanent, dynamic, warm and loving, intelligent power which energizes universal being and becoming.

For the road to the solar-age future is by way of the emergence of an altogether new kind of humanoid, who can consciously experience herself or himself as the individualized manifestation of the cosmic divine in earthly form, while joyously partaking in the mightily majestic ongoing phenomenon of the materialization of spirit. This new humanity will fully feel itself to be an expression of spirit working in and thru the forces of psycho-social development, to provide a proper nervous system for the terrestrial web of life.

So far as our human world is concerned, all this will involve a revolution so fundamental and so thorough-going that its very nature lies wholly beyond the extremely narrow experience and conceptualizing capacity of primitive conventional humankind. Indeed, the coming evolutionary leap forward will require the emergence of truly cosmic humans, whose destiny is to become moral and spiritual giants. This is the natural and proper direction for the human phenomenon to take, because it will be only through the appearance of such developed persons that the appropriate psycho-social form—which the current terrestrial situation demands—can be actualized in practice. Then, once this New Humanity is in being, spirit will be able to work through it on an altogether higher plane in furthering the continued exploration of itself in material form. So the epochal terrestrial revolution now in the making is at the same time a cosmic overleap of utterly stupendous proportions.

All this is going to be brought about through the forces of terrestrial evolution. The future of the earth and its web of life as well as the future of the whole solar system demands nothing less than this. As things stand, technocratic man currently blocks this future course of true psycho-social progress. But it is only a matter of time before his morally insane kind is swept into the trashcan of historical extinction, leaving nothing more behind than a mere blur on the evolutionary annals of our human kind. So beware! Beware all those of the technocratic mold! Beware of the utterly merciless nemesis that is coming!

And let no one else be in any doubt about our true function and true purpose as human beings in the evolution of the cosmos! For we have been brought into being not to fritter away our lives in useless doings, but to transcend our ordinary earthly selves by becoming cosmic beings whose home is the very universe itself. In the not too distant future, solar age humans—as the cosmic crusaders looking back upon the whole evolutionary history of humanoid forms—will see our mean and squalid and petty present as just a brief occurrence in a long drawn-out barbaric past, before the beginning of real human history and the advent of a genuine civilization on planet earth!

Michael Tobin

BIBLIOGRAPHY

THE AUTHOR AND PUBLISHER regret that so few excellent books, pamphlets, and magazine articles referred to in the text can now be found in print. However, we have made a complete list of everything referred to in this book, and have placed an asterisk (*) in front of references that were located in Books in Print, 1990. If you come across any others in a used bookstore or on someone's shelf, or even in a library somewhere, and it's not too much trouble, please send the correct information to me at the publisher's address. Thanks. I had all of them and more once, but many moves and ever leaner baggage left me only with their good inspiration, and perhaps a bit cleaner, wiser, and freer.

ABRAMOWSKI, DR. O.L.M. *Fruitarian Diet and Physical Rejuvenation.*
*ACCIARDO, MARCIA. *Light Eating for Survival.* Twenty-first Century Publications, 1978.
Acres, U.S.A. Magazine (monthly). Available from: P.O. Box 9547, Kansas City, MO 64133. All-around, the most intelligent periodical published today in America.
ALDER, VERA STANLEY. *From the Mundane to the Magnificent.*
ANDREWS, SHEILA. *The No-Cook Fruitarian Recipe Book.* Newbury Books.
*BAKER, ELSWORTH. *Man in the Trap.* New York: Avon, 1979.
BEALLE, MORRIS. *The Drug Story.*
BEAN, ORSON. *Me and the Orgone.*
BERNARD, RAYMOND. *The Mysteries of Human Reproduction.* Omangod Press.
BIELER, M.D., HENRY. *Food is Your Best Medicine.*
BRANDT, JOHANNA. *The Grape Cure.*
BURROUGHS, STANLEY. *Healing for the Age of Enlightenment.* 8905 Crater Hill Rd., Ophir, CA.
*CARPENTER, EDWARD. *Civilization: Its Cause and Cure.* Whittier, CA: Greenleaf.
*COUSENS, GABRIEL. *Spiritual Nutrition and the Rainbow Diet,* 1986. Available from: Cassandra Press, P.O. Box 2044, Boulder, CO 80306.
*DIAMOND, HARVEY & MARILYN. *Fit for Life.* New York: Warner, 1985.
*DIAMOND, JOHN. *Your Body Doesn't Lie.* New York: Warner, 1980.
EDDS, KEVIN. *How to Live 100's of Years.*
EHRET, ARNOLD. *The Definitive Cure of Chronic Constipation.* 19 Babcock Place, Yonkers, NY: Ehret Literature Publishing Co.
EHRET, ARNOLD. *Mucusless Diet Healing System.* 19 Babcock Place, Yonkers, NY: Ehret Literature Publishing Co.
EHRET, ARNOLD. *Rational Fasting.* 19 Babcock Place, Yonkers, NY: Ehret Literature Publishing Co.
EHRET, ARNOLD. *Roads to Health and Happiness.* 19 Babcock Place, Yonkers, NY: Ehret Literature Publishing Co.
EHRET, ARNOLD. *Thus Speaketh the Stomach.* 19 Babcock Place, Yonkers, NY: Ehret Literature Publishing Co.

FRY, T.C. The Myth of Medicine.

GOLDSTEIN, DR. JACK. Triumph Over Disease through Fasting and Natural Diet.

*GOODMAN, LINDA. Star Signs. St. Martin's, 1988.

*GREGORY, DICK. Dick Gregory's Natural Diet for Folks Who Eat: Cooking with Mother Nature. New York: Harper & Row, 1974.

GRIFFITH, KYLE. Spiritual Revolution: War in Heaven. Palo Alto, CA: S/R Press, P.O. Box 60327, Palo Alto, CA 94306.

*GRUNDY, JULIA M. Ten Days in the Light of Akka. Wilmette, IL: Bahai Publ. Trust, 1979.

HAMAKER, JOHN & WEAVER, DON. The Survival of Civilization, 1982. Available from: Hamaker-Weaver, Box 1961, Burlingame, CA 94010.

HARRIS, W. & MACDONALD, N. F. Is Menstruation Necessary? Life Science Publishers.

Healthful Living Magazine (monthly). Available from: Life Science, 6600 Burleson Rd., P.O. Box 17128, Austin, TX 78760.

HOFFMAN, JAY M. Hunza: Fifteen Secrets of the Healthiest and Oldest Living People. Escondido, CA: Professional Press, 1968.

HONIBALL, ESSIE. I Live on Fruit.

HOVANNESSIAN, ARSHAVIRTER. Raw Eating.

HURNARD, HANNAH. Fruitarianism: Compassionate Way to Transformed Health.

*JACKINS, HARVEY. Benign Reality. Seattle: Rational Island Publishers, 1981.

*JANOV, ARTHUR. The Primal Scream. New York: Putnam, 1981.

KELDER, PETER. The Five Rites of Rejuvenation. Garberville, CA: Borderland Sciences.

KELDER, PETER. Ancient Secret of the Fountain of Youth. Gig Harbor, WA: Harbor Press.

KIRSCHNER, M.D., H.E. Live Food Juices. Monrovia, CA: Kirschner Publications, 1957.

KIRSCHNER, M.D., H.E. Nature's Healing Grasses. Riverside, CA: H.C. White Publications, 1975.

KROK, MORRIS. Fruit, the Food and Medicine of Man.

KROK, MORRIS. Kindred Soul.

*KULVINSKAS, VIKTORAS. Life in the 21st Century. 21st Century Publications, P.O. Box 64, Woodstock Valley, CT 06282.

KULVINSKAS, VIKTORAS. Love Your Body: Live Food Recipes. Wethersfield, CT: Omangod Press, 1972.

KULVINSKAS, VIKTORAS. New Age Directory.

*KULVINSKAS, VIKTORAS & TARCA, JR., RICHARD. Survival into the 21st Century. 21st Century Publications, P.O. Box 64, Woodstock Valley, CT 06282.

*LAME DEER. Seeker of Visions. New York: Simon & Schuster, 1972.

*LEONARDO, B. & GREGORY, S.J. Conquering AIDS Now! 1986. Available from: Tree of Life Publications, 513 Wilshire Blvd., #244, Santa Monica, CA 90401.

LOVEWISDOM, DR. JOHNNY. *The Healing God Spell of St. John.* Available from: International University of Natural Living, Casilla 237, Loja, Equador.

LOVEWISDOM, DR. JOHNNY. *How to Grow and Eat the Vitarian Fruit-Salad Diet.* (See above address.)

MAE, E. & LOEFFLER, C. *How I Conquered Cancer Naturally.* Eugene, OR: Harvest House, 1976.

MITCHELL, TERESA. *Roads to Health and Happiness.* 19 Babcock Pl, Yonkers, NY: Ehret Literature Publishing Co.

*NOLFI, DR. K. *The Miracles of Living Foods.* Parsons, WV: McClain, 1981. Available from: New Medical Books, P.O. Box 2357, Dept. 51, Elkins, WV.

*ORR, L. & RAY, S. *Rebirthing in the New Age.* Berkeley, CA: Celestial Arts, 1987.

PEARSON, R.B. *Pasteur Plagiarist Imposter!*

PHILLIPS, D.A. *From Soil to Psyche.* Aquarian, 27 Power Ave., Alexandria, NSW 2015, Australia.

*RAJNEESH, BHAGWAN SHREE. *Meditation: The Art of Ecstasy.* New York: Harper & Row, 1978.

*REICH, WILHELM. *The Function of Orgasm: Selected Writings.* New York: Farrar, Straus & Giroux, 1986.

REUSCH, HANS. *Naked Empress, or the Great Medical Hoax.*

*SHELTON, HERBERT. *Hygenic Care of Children.* Tampa, FL: Natural Hygiene, 1970.

*SHELTON, HERBERT. *The Science and Fine Art of Fasting.* Tampa, FL: Natural Hygiene, 1978.

*SHELTON, HERBERT. *Fasting Can Save Your Life.* Tampa, FL: Natural Hygiene, 1981.

*SHELTON, HERBERT. *The Science and Fine Art of Food and Nutrition.* Tampa, FL: Natural Hygiene, 1984.

*SHELTON, HERBERT. *The Original Natural Hygiene Weight Loss Diet Book.* New Canaan, CT: Keats, 1986.

Soil Remineralization Magazine. Available from: 152 South Street, Northampton, MA 01060.

SWANGKEE, RAY. *RQLZ for Fasting.* The Peacock, Angel Ridge, King's Mountain, KY 40442.

*SZEKELY, E.B. *Biogenic Reducing: The Wonder Week—The Healthy Way—A Pound a Day.* San Diego, CA: IBS International, 1967.

*SZEKELY, E.B. *The Essene Gospel of Peace, Books 1-4.* San Diego, CA: IBS International, 1981.

TOBE, JOHN. *The Golden Treasury of Natural Health Knowledge.*

TOBE, JOHN. *Hunza: Adventures in a Land of Paradise.*

*WIGMORE, DR. ANN. *Be Your Own Doctor—A Positive Guide to Natural Living.* Garden City Park, NY: Avery, 1983. You may also contact the Ann Wigmore Foundation, 196 Commonwealth Ave., Boston, MA 02116.

*YOGANANDA, PARAMAHANSA. *The Autobiography of a Yogi.* Los Angeles: Self-Realization Fellowship, 1981.